FLOPPY DISK FEVER

THE CURIOUS AFTERLIVES OF A FLEXIBLE MEDIUM

TEXT - NIEK HILKMANN
DESIGN - THOMAS WALSKAAR
FOREWORD - LORI EMERSON
MEDIA GLOSSARY - JASON CURTIS

ONOMATOPEE 197

CONTENTS

'The mere image of the floppy disk floats nearly unnoticed throughout our entire digital ecosystem.'

FOREWORD:

FLOPPY DISKS AND A CURABLE KIND OF MELANCHOLIA

LORI EMERSON (CA/US) is an Associate Professor in the Department of English and the Intermedia Arts, Writing and Performance Program at the University of Colorado, Boulder. She is also the Founding Director of the Media Archaeology Lab. Emerson writes about media poetics and the history of computing, media archaeology, media theory, and digital humanities.

In the following text she reflects on the potential dangers and productive possibilities of nostalgia that unavoidably comes with floppy disks. Should we approach obsolete media with caution?

Totally unmoored from its not-yet-obsolete material existence as a read/write medium, the mere image of the floppy disk floats nearly unnoticed throughout our entire digital ecosystem. Meanwhile, and not unrelated, tech companies press on in their mission to practically eradicate computers as such – or, rather, our awareness of there being programmable computers at all.[1] Part of how they do this is through a relentless phasing out of tangibility, as every year we say goodbye to yet another port, and an increasing reliance on skeuomorphs, derivative objects that retain unnecessary attributes from their original form, like the image of the floppy disk that lives on your computer's 'desktop'. Who needs the ability to have a disk you can hold in your hand and use to read, write, and share files when you can replace it with the image of a disk that leads you inevitably to the cloud?

Even George Basalla, the historian who coined the term skeuomorph in 1988, could not see any utility in it. As he saw it, skeuomorphs were 'an element of design or structure that serves little or no purpose in the artifact fashioned from the new material but was essential to the object made from the original material.'[2] But given how much twenty-first century tech relies on them, it seems that one of the main purposes of a skeuomorph must be to remember when we both knew and believed in the function of a given thing. In other words, what if the image of the floppy disk is the designer's unwitting paean to that time period, sometime between the 1970s and the 1990s, when we had a sense about how our computers worked? When we knew where our data lived and we also knew who (not what) we were sharing our data with? As such, as long as it doesn't disappear into overfamiliarity, the skeuomorph is a potentially meaningful vehicle for nostalgia. As long as we actually see it as such, we can still remember the past and reimagine an alternative future.

To be clear, one need not have lived through the past to feel nostalgic about it and to long for something other than what we have now. I have witnessed it first-hand in the Media Archaeology Lab – a place that I and about a dozen other students, staff, and volunteers, born anywhere from the 1970s to the 2000s, unironically call 'home'. Here, anyone at all, of any age and any background, can come in and have hands-on access to still-functioning media from the late nineteenth century to now. You can test out a camera from the 1890s, crank an Edison Diamond Disc phonograph player from 1912, flip switches on an Altair 8800b computer from 1976, or play Oregon Trail on an Apple IIe from 1983. For years, since the lab first opened in 2009, we have ourselves wondered why everything in the lab is so delightful to look at and play with. It must be that the place is saturated

---

1   Lori Emerson, 'Interfaced', *Further Reading*, Oxford University Press, New York, 2020, p. 350-62.
2   George Basalla, *The Evolution of Technology*, Cambridge University Press, Cambridge, 1989, p. 107.

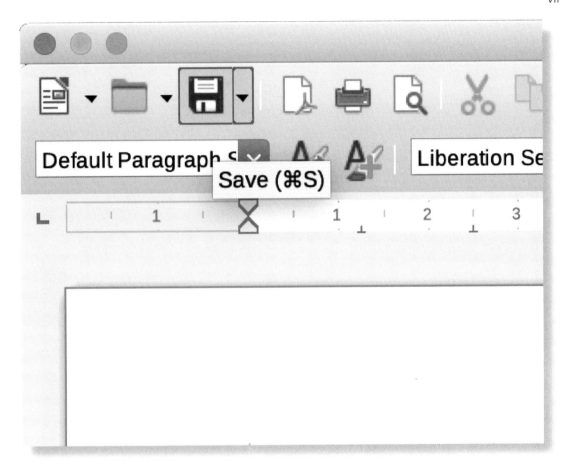

1.1 – The skeuomorphic floppy disk save icon as it can be found within text editors. Source: Floppy Disk Fever

1.2 – The Media Archelogy Lab in 2021. Photo: MAL

with nostalgia – but what does that even mean when young people in their late teens and early 20s also seem to be overcome with the same feelings of homey delight when they first walk in the door? 'Wooooow... is this a computer? How do you turn it on? What does it do? What do you call this? Is this a typewriter? What does it mean when the bell rings?' And then, sometimes after an hour or even two hours of concentrated typing, fiddling with buttons and switches, sighs of wonder and longing (and also bearing in mind they almost always first come to the lab as part of a class requirement), they announce, 'I have to text my parents about this – they're going to be blown away... Can I come back this week and hang out?'

While the computers and game consoles from the 1970s are usually objects of the most admiration, what often remains unseen, unremarked on, and unacknowledged until there's seemingly nothing left in the lab to ogle at, are the bins, boxes, trays, enve-lopes, and cabinets full of floppy disks of all sizes – some with handwritten labels, some imprinted with corporate logos, many com-pletely blank. Rightly or wrongly, we feel we have such an abundance of floppy disks that we have started giving them away to particu-larly enthusiastic visitors, one of whom was incredulous to be holding a mythical 'floppy disk' in his hands. Waving it in the air, he exclaimed, 'I had no idea they were floppy!' With this strange object from a foreign land in their backpacks, an object which they are almost certainly unable to use as the read/

write medium it was meant for, these young people walk out of the lab seemingly buoyed with both longing for a world they never lived in and hope for a future world that is unlike the one they're in right now. They don't need to hear a lecture from me or the staff of the MAL about the trajectory of computing to immediately understand that the current paired practices of blackboxing devices and making them functionally obsolete within just a few years of their making is destroying the planet and its inhabitants. Likewise, they also understand that the inhabitants of the MAL are not proselytising a return to a Golden Age. Floppy disks and old computing are not the answers to our problems – but they are, as I write above, vehicles to rethink what's pragmatically and philosophically possible.

One of the contributors to this book, Nick Gentry, expresses a similar sentiment – while he uses floppies as raw material for art, he also acknowledges that they are 'cultural artifacts that remind us who we are and where we are going'. Similarly, Clint Basinger thinks of his YouTube channel on retro tech and classic gaming as a 'modern look at nostalgia. I sometimes describe it as looking forward by looking back'. And while they don't frame it in terms of attempted time travel or nostalgia, Florian Cramer and Foone Turing acknowledge that the floppy disk's limited speed, storage, and reliability points to lost pasts – to a time when limitations were clear, known, accepted, and embraced as a challenge. By contrast, what are the limita-tions of the cloud when we don't know where it is, who or what has access to our data, and we may not have read the 9 000 word long terms of service (or at least that is the current word count of Apple's iCloud TOS)?

However, even though nearly all of this book's contributors' experiences with floppy disks and nostalgia are framed in positive terms, as has been our experience in and around the Media Archaeology Lab, it is still important to bear in mind that nostalgia has – and for good reason – long been associated with being at best an affliction and at worse a delusion. 'Nostalgia' was first used by the Swiss physician Johannes Hofer to refer to a medical condition 'character-ised by an incapacitating longing for one's motherland'.[3] Those of us who grew up in the 1980s and the era of postmodernism learned to think of nostalgia as something that ought to be vigorously fought against. Fredric Jameson, for example, argued that nostalgia signals a loss of historicity and an evasion of the present for the sake of a 'mesmerized fascination in lavish images of specific generational pasts'.[4] While Jameson was writing specifically about Philip K. Dick, the same could be said of any populist movement from the twentieth and twenty-first centuries that's based on a notion of a fictional Golden Age. Most recently, we have lived through all kinds of deeply

disturbing, nostalgia-based sloganeering from the U.S.'s 'Make America Great Again' to Brazil's 'Brazil above everything, God above everyone', Greece's 'So we can rid this land of filth', and Denmark's even more sinister-sounding 'You know what we stand for'. As Svetlana Boym astutely points out:

> The danger of nostalgia is that it tends to confuse the actual home and the imaginary one. In extreme cases it can create a phantom homeland, for the sake of which one is ready to die or kill. Unreflected nostalgia breeds monsters. Yet the sentiment itself, the mourning of displacement and temporal irreversibility, is at the very core of the modern condition.[5]

For those invested in the dangerous form of nostalgia, 'home', as they imagine it, never existed. But, for those invested in using the present to reflect on the past, using the past to reflect on the present, and using past and present to reshape the future, nostalgia can be both productive and powerful. Katharina Niemeyer reminds us that nostalgia is a:

> Collective way of relieving the pain of space, time, and personal loss. It makes it possible to confront the irreversibility of time, our finiteness,

3   Felipe De Brigard, 'Nostalgia doesn't need real memories – an imagined past works as well', *Aeon Essays*, accessed 20 July 2020, https://aeon.co/essays/nostalgia-doesnt-need-real-memories-an-imagined-past-works-as-well

4   Fredric Jameson, *Postmodernism, or, The Logic of Late Capitalism*, Duke University Press, Durham, NC, 1991, p. 296.

5   Svetlana Boym, *The Future of Nostalgia*, Basic Books, New York, 2002, p. xvi.

and nostalgia lets humans (re-) connect with each other.[6]

Somewhat surprisingly, once one leaves the realm of humanities and wanders into the fields of psychology, neuroscience, and cognitive science, one discovers there are hundreds of studies that show all kinds of benefits to nostalgia: nostalgic memories can foster optimism;[7] nostalgia is a source of comfort in adverse weather;[8] nostalgia can be used as a way to combat ageism;[9] and, overall, nostalgia helps people 'attain a more meaningful life, protects from existential threat, and contributes to psychological equanimity.'[10] All of these things are borne out by the interviews in this book and certainly I have witnessed the positive potential of nostalgia myself.

If Gertrude Stein had lived in the 1980s she might have said 'A floppy is a floppy is a floppy' – not because any floppy (or rose, for that matter) is as ordinary and replaceable as any other but because they are each remarkable and singular objects that open up, in nearly innumerable ways, alternative ways of thinking and being. A floppy is a floppy is a floppy.

6   Katharina Niemeyer, 'The Power of Nostalgia: About the role and place of media and communication (scholars) in nostalgia studies, Nostalgias e mídia: no caleidoscópio do tempo'. *E-papers Serviços Editoriais Ltda.*, 2019, p. 23.

7   Marios Biskas, 'A Prologue to Nostalgia: Savouring Creates Nostalgic Memories that Foster Optimism'. *Cognition and Emotion* 33:3, 417-27.

8   Wignand A. P. van Tilburg, 'Adverse Weather Evokes Nostalgia'. *Personality and Social Psychology Bulletin* 44:7, 984-95.

9   Rhiannon N. Turner, 'Fighting Ageism through Nostalgia'. *European Journal of Social Psychology* 48:2, 196-208.

10 Constantine Sedikides, 'Finding Meaning in Nostalgia'. *Review of General Pyschology* 22:1, 48-61.

'Figuring out what happened to the medium and how we relate to it after its presumed downfall opens the door to an almost infinite amount of topics, all worthy of further investigation.'

PREFACE:

IN STATE OF FLUX – BEYOND PILLOWS AND COASTERS

NIEK HILKMANN (NL) is a Rotterdam based artist, musician, and researcher with a background in Media Design, Art History and Visual Culture. Besides being responsible for organising various floppy-centered events as part of Floppy Totaal, he is also one of the main editors of Floppy Disk Fever.

This introduction addresses the motives behind the book and the many afterlives of contemporary floppy culture. Where to start with such a broad topic?

Tell someone that you're writing a book on floppy disks and you usually get a chuckle in return. There is something so overfamiliar about the format, that it somehow transcends space and time, with its meaning being mostly determined by association. For many the floppy disk is primarily a symbol of retro kitsch, a commercialised relic from the past that outstayed its welcome by re-appearing as tacky merchandise, such as floppy shaped pillows and coasters. Others immediatly pick up on the element of nostalgia attached to the medium and praise or write off the floppy in this light. However, both approaches disregard the full meaning of the floppy's residual afterlife in the twenty first century and oversimplify its rather unique place in history.

For me, the floppy disk is the most prevalent and eye-catching obsolescent consumer-oriented electronic data carrier of the twentieth century. It went from being rather ubiquitous to an obscure relic over the course of a mere 50 years. Figuring out what happened to the medium and how we relate to it after its presumed downfall opens doors to an almost infinite number of topics, all worthy of further investigation. While preparing for the interviews found in this book, we came across various texts that were specifically oriented towards floppy disks in the context of nostalgia,[1] obsolescence,[2] and media history.[3] Rarer still were the studies that approached its status as a contemporary cultural phenomenon.[4] There are many questions that remain mostly unanswered.

What does it mean for a medium to keep on trucking after it hit its perceived expiration date? Is there anything we can learn from its continued presence today? And can it still find new uses that its original designers never anticipated?

Within the context of profit-driven planned obsolescence, it is important to inquire after the reuse and repurposing of 'obsolete' technologies. With electronic waste piles growing larger and more conspicuous every year, how do artists and consumers engage with older media? The ideology behind redundancy can be questioned through the contemporary use and creative repurposing of outdated technology, of which many floppy related examples can be found in this book. This methodology goes beyond mere nostalgia. Those who (re)introduce older technology in our current times often combine media from the past with contemporary ones. The result is a hybrid cultural expression that reveals the necessity to question the way in which technological development gets framed, both by media-centred research and popular culture.

1   Katharina Niemeyer, *Media and Nostalgia – Yearning for the Past, Present and Future,* Palgrave Macmillan, London, 2014.
2   B. Tischleder, S. Wasserman, *Cultures of Obsolescence: History, Materiality, and the Digital Age,* Palgrave Macmillan, London, 2015.
3   Mark J.P. Wolf, *The Routledge Companion to Media Technology and Obsolescence,* Routledge, Abingdon, Oxfordshire, 2018.
4   Matthew Kirschenbaum, *Poor Black Square, 'The Routledge Companion to Media Technology and Obsolescence',* Routledge, Abingdon, Oxfordshire, 2018, p. 296-310.

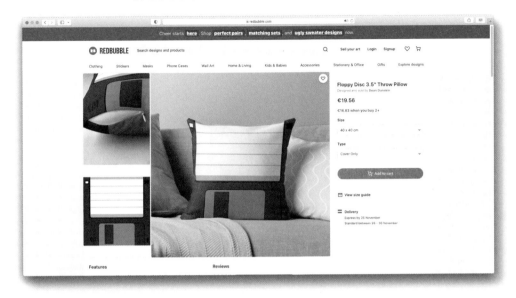

2.1 – A floppy disk shaped pillow, ready for purchase on RedBubble. Source: redbubble.com

It was this idea that led to the initial formation of Floppy Totaal, a recurrent festival since 2014 organised at WORM, the institute of avant-garde recreation in Rotterdam, the Netherlands. During these events a variety of international artists, musicians, hackers, designers, and researchers were invited to showcase their contemporary floppy related projects. It was here that I first got into contact with many of the people interviewed for this book, including Jason Scott and Adam Frankiewicz. There were also numerous great artists who aren't interviewed but deserve special mention, such as Sascha Müller, Kai Nabuko, Remute, and many others. The events grew larger with each edition, and before long there was something that could

be called a Floppy Totaal team. This included Thomas Walskaar and Lídia Pereira who both contributed to this book. After the first three editions of the festival, we wanted to expand our original vision beyond its event-based format; the time had come to capture the contemporary spirit of the floppy on paper.

To achieve this, we chose to interview a broad range of floppy enthusiasts and capture their views and thoughts. We handpicked these according to discipline, from floppy painting with Nick Gentry to floppy filmmaking with Florian Cramer. Of course, this still does not fully cover the entire world of the floppy disk today, but it does give a first taste of what is a much larger phenomenon than one might

2.2 - One of the posters for the 2015 edition of Floppy Totaal, created by Kai Nabuko. Source: Floppy Disk Fever

2.3 - The poster for Floppy Totaal: Magnetic Flux (2019), designed by Thomas Walskaar. Source: Floppy Disk Fever

suspect. For instance, Adam Frankiewiecz with his Pionierska Records label, is an example of floppy disk music, which is a sub-scene larger enough for a book of its own.[5] The same can be said about Clint Basinger who represents the world of floppy YouTubers and retro content creators. Our hope is that by including this wide variety of approaches, the many sides of the medium come to light without leaving too much behind.

This does not mean that there aren't any absences or overlaps. From a look at the list of interviewees it is evident that all are from the west (either North American or European) and ostensibly male. It proved rather difficult to broaden up this demographic without resorting to measures that might paint an unrealistic image of the subject. Conclusions can be drawn from this, but this introduction will remain free from any bold claims or cultural analyses. Our goal is mainly to provide a fair view on what is currently going on in the world of floppy disks and, by extension, residual media. The result provides insight into a particular subject within an historical context. Its main methodological question is what this specificity can offer us as media historians, researchers, or anyone else interested in the topic.

As such, we prepared the interviews with a common set of themes in mind. For instance, the interviewee's take on nostalgia, the future of the floppy disk, and their own history with the medium are each tackled multiple times. By doing so, we hope to offer different viewpoints across various disciplines on subjects pertaining to the medium. This does not mean that we do not discuss the interviewee's individual work and ideas any further. Sometimes these parts are actually the most revealing. The combination of all these different approaches to the same medium has the potential to give this book an added value and reveal something that might not otherwise be apparent.

We want these interviews to be enjoyable and readable within and outside of the floppy disk community. That is why we included a media glossary by Jason Curtis, which came about after our interview with him. This glossary can be a handy tool to refresh one's mind or learn something new. We invite you to read the interviews in any order you like by just picking a topic that interests you from the table of contents. Pulling this book together was quite a trip, and we hope we were able to do justice to such a curious and flexible medium. There's only one way to find out – by flipping through the pages and getting sucked into the many afterlives of the floppy disk!

---

5   Kai Nabuko most likely published the first anthology of floppy disk music reviews with his print-on-demand *Yeah I Know It Sucks: Underground Music Reviews Vol. 1 and Vol. 2.*

'When people ask me: "Why are you into floppy disks today?" the answer is simple: "Because I forgot to get out of the business." '

THE LAST MAN IN THE BUSINESS

TOM PERSKY (US) is the 'last man standing in the floppy disk business'. He is the founder of floppydisk.com, a US-based company, dedicated to the selling and recycling of floppy disks. Other services the company provides include disk transfers, a recycling program, and selling used and/or broken floppy disks to artists worldwide. All this makes floppydisk.com a key player in the contemporary floppy scene.

We met Tom to discuss the current state of the floppy disk industry and the perks and challenges of running a business like his in the 2020s. What has changed and what remains the same?

Floppy Totaal (FT): Hi Tom, it's great to finally meet the founder of floppydisks.com. We'd love to know a little more about your company. Let's start with the obvious: how did you end up with the domain for floppydisks.com?

TP: Nice to meet you too! I think it happened during the early days of the Internet, around 1990. At the time we believed that the Internet should be free and that cybersquatting was a crime. One day somebody contacted me and asked if I wanted to buy the domain for $1 000 I felt it was an outrage. I told my wife I would not participate in this kind of cybercrime, but she took out a chequebook and got the domain name instantly. This went totally against my principles, but thankfully my wife is much smarter than I am.

FT: Were you already selling floppy disks at the time?

TP: 20 years ago I was actually in the floppy disk duplication business. Not in a million years did I think I would ever sell blank floppy disks. Duplicating disks in the 1980s and early 1990s was as good as printing money. It was unbelievably profitable. I only started selling blank copies organically over time. You could still go down to any office supply store, or any computer store to buy them. Why would you try to find me, when you could just buy disks off the shelf? But then these larger companies stopped carrying them or went out of business and people came to us. So here I am, a small company with a floppy disk inventory, and I find myself to be a worldwide supplier of this product. My business, which used to be 90% CD and DVD duplication, is now 90% selling blank floppy disks. It's shocking to me.

FT: How did your business come about?

TP: I started out as a tax lawyer in Washington, DC. I became involved with a software company in California that was doing unique tax calculations. I left my practice with Price Waterhouse and moved to California with a little firm called Time Value Software. This was in the early 90s. I had no software background whatsoever, but I had a good tax background. The idea was that I would use my tax expertise to work with programmers, and develop better software for tax practitioners. I did that for about ten years. In the process, we developed a couple of different software applications. In the 90s the way you would distribute software would be by floppy disk, either on a 5.25-inch or a 3.5-inch disk. At one point we did a gigantic deal with a US payroll company for which we needed to copy hundreds of thousands of disks. We sent the work out to a third party who did the duplication for us. That was okay, but expensive, and it took a lot of time. The quality also wasn't quite what we wanted it to be. So the next time we decided to do the floppy duplication in-house and we got our own equipment. This way we could distribute our software to our customers ourselves.

FT: How did this software company become a duplication company?

TP: Because we were a tax-oriented company and had specific tax filing deadlines we only used our duplication equipment once every quarter. For 89 days in a row, the machines would be unused and then, on a single day, we would punch out thousands and thousands of floppy disks. At some point, I looked at the machines and how they were unused for so much of the time, and I had the idea to take in other people's laundry. If the machines were there, I could do the duplication and probably make a little extra money. I started spending an hour a day on it, then I spent two hours, then four, and eventually I hired somebody else to do it. Before I knew it I had a software duplication company that was working alongside the software company. We basically spun that little business out and I ended up creating floppydisks.com. We now have three employees and continue to do CD and DVD duplication, but most of our revenue comes from selling blank floppy disks.

FT: Where does this focus on floppy disks come from? Why not work with another medium?

TP: In the beginning I figured we would do floppy disks, but never CDs. Eventually, we got into CDs and I said we'd never do DVDs. A couple of years went by and I started duplicating DVDs. Now I'm also duplicating USB drives. You can see from this conversation that I'm not exactly a person with great vision. I just follow what our customers want us to do. When people ask me: 'Why are you into floppy disks today?' the answer is: 'Because I forgot to get out of the business.' Everybody else in the world looked at the future and came to the conclusion that this was a dying industry. Because I'd already bought all my equipment and inventory, I thought I'd just keep this revenue stream. I stuck with it and didn't try to expand. Over time the total number of floppy users has gone down. However, the number of people who provided the product went down even faster. If you look at those two curves, you see that there is a growing market share for the last man standing in the business, and that man is me.

FT: How many floppy disks do you have in stock at the moment?

TP: Not as many as I'd like, something in the order of half a million. We carry all the different flavours; 3.5-inch, 5.25-inch, 8-inch and some rather rare diskettes. Another thing that happened organically was the start of our floppy disk recycling service. We give people the opportunity to send us floppy disks and we recycle them, rather than put them into a landfill. The sheer volume of floppy disks we get in has really surprised me, it's sometimes a 1 000 disks a day.

FT: Where do these disks come from? Are they from all over the world?

3.1 – Tom Persky at work in his office. Screenshot of *Where Floppy Disks are Still in Use*, a video by Great Big Story (2015) Source: YouTube

TP: Well, I kind of discourage international shipping, because if you're really doing a recycling service, you don't want people to put stuff on a jet plane. It's also just too expensive. We don't pay for shipping, providing instead what I would call a reasonable shipping offset. If you shop around and find the cheapest possible shipping, we'll cover it. Of the 1 000 disks we get in every day 100 might be brand new and 900 of them may have labels on them. With all these packages coming in on a daily basis, it is Christmas here every day.

FT: **What type of floppy disk is most in demand? And which is the most valuable?**

TP: The most in demand is the standard 1.44 MB, 3.5-inch blank floppy disk. I would say that the most valuable are currently the 720KB double density disks. Of course, there are specialty 8-inch disks, for which there is a very small demand and of which we only have a small inventory. They're absolutely irreplaceable. The same could be said about quad density, 5.25-inch disks.

FT: **You mentioned the number of companies still providing floppy disks has substantially decreased. Are there still any companies left that produce them?**

TP: I would say my last buy from a manufacturer was about ten or twelve years ago. Back then I made the decision to buy a large quantity, a couple of million disks,

and we've basically been living off of that inventory ever since. From time to time, we get very lucky. About two years ago a guy called me up and said: 'My grandfather has all this floppy junk in the garage and I want it out. Will you take it?' Of course I wanted to take it off his hands. So, we went back and forth and negotiated what would be a fair price. Without going into specifics, he ended up with two things that he wanted: an empty garage and a sum of money. I ended up with around 50 000 floppy disks and that's a good deal. Everybody felt richer and happier at the end of the transaction. It's the genius of capitalism. Sometimes I also get a company that's cleaning out a warehouse and they find pallets of floppy disks. They figure out through my site that I still buy them and contact me. There's a constant flow. I expect to be in this business for at least another four years or something like that.

FT: **It sounds like there is a finite number of floppy disks available. Is this ever a problem?**

TP: Well, I once got a request from the Netherlands for half a million floppy disks and I had to tell them that I simply didn't have that kind of inventory. Plus, I have two competing goals here. I have a lot of customers for whom I have provided inventory and services for years and years. They helped me build my business and they've helped me pay my mortgage and employees. I want to continue to provide goods and services to these people, so selling out my inventory would not be a good idea. Another thing is that I don't know what my inventories are worth. I know that ten years ago I bought floppy disks for eight to 12 cents apiece. If I was buying a container of a million disks, I could probably get them for eight cents, but what are they worth today? In the last ten years they've gone from ten cents to one dollar apiece, and now you can sell a 720KB double density disks for two dollars. I just don't know what the market will do. It's very hard to run a business when you don't know what your product is worth. Also, who's going to buy the product?

FT: Who are your main customers at the moment?

TP: The customers that are the easiest to provide for are the hobbyists – people who want to buy ten, 20 or maybe 50 floppy disks. However, my biggest customers, and the place where most of the money comes from, are the industrial users. These are people who use floppy disks as a way to get information in and out of a machine. Imagine its 1990, and you're building a big industrial machine of one kind or another. You design it to last 50 years and you'd want to use the best technology available. At the time this was a 3.5-inch floppy disk. Take the airline industry for example. Probably half of the air fleet in the world today is more than 20 years old and still uses floppy disks in some of the avionics. That's a huge consumer. There's also medical equipment, which requires floppy disks to get the

information in and out of medical devices. The biggest customer of all is probably the embroidery business. Thousands and thousands of machines that use floppy disks were made for this, and they still use these. There are even some industrial companies that still use Sony Mavica cameras to take photographs. The vast majority of what I sell is for these industrial uses, but there is a significant hobbyist element to it as well.

FT: I wonder, if there is still a demand for floppy disks in the industrial world, why would the manufacturers stop producing them?

TP: People tend to think about floppy disks in the same way as CDs and DVDs. To produce these, you only have to pour plastic in one end of a large machine, and you're getting CDs or DVDs out at the other end. Even though this might already look like a complex process, it's nothing compared to the manufacturing of a floppy disk. A floppy disk has perhaps nine unique components. There's the plastic moulding, the cookie, a shutter, a spring, etc. Maybe you can do eight out of these nine things, but as I always say, when you're 95% done you're only halfway there. You need all the pieces for the complete product. The amount of effort it would take to recreate a manufacturing line for all of the pieces that go into a floppy would be virtually impossible. We've done it before, of course, but now the demand is simply not there. Plus, in time, all the industrial machines, all the airplanes that still use floppy disks,

3.2 – The floppy disk duplication machine setup. Photo: Tom Persky

are eventually going to be replaced. So why would you want to spend $25 million to tool up a factory to see if you can manufacture the floppy cookie that nobody has made in 25 years? People have been living off of inventory for five or ten years now. Floppy disks were a very specialised piece of technology with a very difficult manufacturing process. Compared to this, a CD looks like a piece of junk. When people ask me why I can't manufacture floppy disks myself, I say I'm missing only one material: it's called unobtainium.

FT: You speak quite highly of the floppy disk. I wonder, have you formed a personal bond with the medium over the years? What do floppy disks mean to you?

TP: To me, the floppy disk is a highly refined, technical, stable, not very hackable, way to get relatively small amounts of data where you want it. I grew up in the days of the Sneakernet and at the time the floppy disk was how we moved information around. It's a really remarkable thing. There's a beauty and elegance to them. I can see how complicated they are, and what an elegant solution they were for their time. I'm not a watch collector, but I have friends who are. The beauty of a finely made watch is something to behold. Even though it might be less reliable than a $19 clock, it is a work of art. Just consider the human effort that went into its making. The same can be said about the floppy disk.

3.3 - Just a small part of the inventory at the floppydisk.com warehouse. Photo: Tom Persky

FT: Do you also use floppy disks in your personal life, outside of the office?

TP: I have to admit, the answer to that question is sadly no. However, I sometimes take them home, because of our transfer service. People send us the disks that they've rediscovered in their drawers. They can no longer use them, but they still want to get to their old address book, PhD thesis, or photographs that are on there. So, somebody might send us five disks with Kodak photographs on them, and we get them off. If we're running behind, I sometimes transfer the data at home while watching American football. You would not believe some of the letters we get back. People see their late grandmother or their baby pictures again and that's very important to them. We're happy to bring these things back. We're not being charitable and we don't need to be congratulated for it, but it is nice to know that we're getting people stuff they really need.

FT: Do you ever worry about data getting lost in this transfer process?

TP: Well, we do the best that we can. We encourage people to store their data in multiple ways. Floppy disks were not intended for long-term storage, neither are CDs, DVDs, or USB drives. If you have important data, it shouldn't be stored only in one place.

FT: There seems to be a new wave of interest in retro media. I was wondering if you see evidence of this in your business, for instance, from people that approach you for new projects that utilise floppy disks?

TP: Well, people mostly buy disks for art projects, not really for building applications. Every once in a while, I'll get a game company that wants to rerelease an old game, but I would say that most of it is for art or for promotions. One of the things that I've seen a lot is the use of floppy disks as badges at conferences. We sold a lot of disks for that, especially the recycled disks that couldn't be reformatted. There is a fallout of about 30%, so we have large amounts of disks that we consider to be unusable. Some of these we might actually have been able to format, but we're just not happy with their quality and reliability.

FT: 30% sounds like a pretty high fail rate. Can you tell us something about the quality difference in certain disks? Which type of floppy is the best and which is the worst to recycle?

TP: In the early years, the manufacturing process for floppy disks was pretty bad. In the middle years, when they made billions and billions of disks, the manufacturing process was great. At the end of the life of the medium, the manufacturing process regressed. I would say that the best disks are the ones made between 1985 and 2000. If they were stored at a decent temperature, they're as good today as they ever were. There's stuff that was made in the last couple of runs that I bought from China and

3.4 - When Tom receives floppy disks, they often arrive at his warehouse in large quantities, as can be seen in this still from Great Big Story (2015). Source: YouTube

half of them were bad. When you think about a manufacturing process that's getting to the end of its life, you have to consider that the testing equipment falls out of calibration. You would have to hire somebody to come in and fix it, but you just can't afford to tool or replace anything. Even though you might lose 30% of your output, you're just going to live with the 70% that you have left. In the end the quality was so bad that people didn't even test the disks anymore. Rather, they just tried to format the disk and if it didn't work, they knew it was bad. They started spitting out as many disks as possible to burn through the remaining stock. I guess they just wanted to get them out and be done with it.

FT: How do you check if the disks you sell are still usable?

TP: When we get the disks in, we do a copy and compare before we send them back out into the world. If it works for us, we're confident that it's going to work in the field. By the way, even in the best days a half percent failure rate was not unheard of. If you bought a 50 pack from the store in the mid 90s, it was very likely that there would be one or two duds and that was actually okay.

FT: Were you ever tempted to jump ship and sell something other than floppies?

TP: No, I'm now 72 years old and I've been a tax lawyer, a software developer, and a CD/DVD duplicator. Some people like Sudoku, some people like crossword puzzles. Me, I just like to get up in the morning, have people ask me questions, and try to solve problems. My business is a little bit of an adventure for me every day.

FT: Do you think that floppy disks have a future?

TP: I would say that floppy disks have a future, but it won't see a revival like Vinyl. People like the idea of the record player and it will be around for a long time as a very niche or cool kind of thing. Floppy disks are going to be a little bit more like buggy whips or typewriters. They're going to be a collectible marvel of their time. Imagine how hard it would be to manufacture a new typewriter today. There are a number of American authors who talk about the fact that they can only write on a typewriter. It's something very important to them that is tied into their artistic genius. I think that floppy disks are going to be a little bit like that. You're not going to be able to replace them. There's this joke in which a three-year-old little girl comes to her father holding a floppy disk in her hand. She says: 'Daddy, Daddy, somebody 3D-printed the save icon'. The floppy disks will be an icon forever.

'I actually wanted to get sued by Hollywood! Maybe somebody from the studios looked at my floppy films and decided that their seven-by-three pixels were not enough reason to sue me. I was really dissapointed.'

THE GORY DETAILS

FLORIAN CRAMER (NL) is a practice-oriented research professor in
21st Century Visual Culture at the Willem de Kooning Academy
in Rotterdam, the Netherlands. Since 2009, he has developed a
habit for creating and distributing films using floppy disks and
has conducted multiple workshops on the subject. By employing
extreme measures of compression he is able to squeeze
entire movies onto the 1.44 MB provided by the medium. The
floppy disk also stood at the center of several of his collabora-
tive film projects as a vehicle for collective constraint.

*We asked Florian about the methodology behind his work
and the potential of the floppy disk as a contemporary
experimental medium. What's the link between
'combinatorial poetics' and 'floppy life cinema'?*

Floppy Totaal (FT): Hello Florian, we're very glad you could find the time for this interview!

Florian Cramer (FC): It's always a pleasure, especially when it's on the subject of floppy disks.

FT: We would like to start by asking you about your background. How would you describe yourself?

FC: That's actually quite a difficult question. Formally I'm a professor at the Willem de Kooning Academy and the Piet Zwart Institute in Rotterdam. In the Netherlands, we have this particular construction of practice-oriented research at art schools. My job is to look at the developments and changes of the overall field of arts and design, making sure that we as an art school are not teaching the art practice of the last century. My focus is on self-organised and DIY forms of artistic practice, and what we can learn from them. That, of course, has a lot to do with floppy disks.

FT: We would like to know more about this link between DIY practices and floppy disks. Is this relationship something contemporary or has it always been there?

FC: Well, the floppy disk was originally invented as a business technology – for business computers and business data exchange – but later it became intrinsically linked with the history of home computing. After audiocassettes it was the first affordable storage medium for home computers in the 1980s and 90s.

FT: Did your personal relationship with home computers also start back then?

FC: Absolutely, I first got in touch with them in 1981, when I was 9 years old. That was the time when the very first affordable home computers became available in Europe. My first home computer was the Sinclair ZX81. You could call it the great grandfather of the Raspberry Pi, because of its simple construction and unrivalled low price, which was €140 if we adjust for inflation. This was a breakthrough, although the computer couldn't do very much. It was essentially a programmable pocket calculator that could be connected to a screen, and which could also display text and monochrome pixel graphics. It had a working memory of only 1 KB. You needed to connect a tape cassette recorder to save and load data. Its memory could be extended from 1 to 16 KB with an external module, which felt like infinite worlds and infinite space at the time. Compare that to the 1440 KB of the floppy disk!

FT: That's at least 87.5 times the memory. When did you start using floppy disks?

FC: The first computer that I had with a built-in floppy drive was the Atari 1040ST, a very strange machine that had the same CPU as the early Amiga and the first Macintosh computers. Its desktop interface was an unsophisticated knockoff of the first-generation Mac, but the underlying operating system more resembled MS DOS. This machine was particularly popular with people who made music, because it was the only one that had a built-in MIDI interface at the time. You could use it for controlling synthesizers.

FT: Did you also use your Atari for this purpose?

FC: Well no, because I didn't have a MIDI synthesizer. However, I did program computer-generated music in BASIC on the 8-bit computer that I had before that. This was even published on cassette tapes at the time. Still, even the Atari ST, which was a more advanced machine that resembled a contemporary personal computer, didn't have a hard drive. All programs and data, everything you loaded, everything you saved, was on a floppy disk. So, I immediately got exposed to the precariousness of the medium. If there was a bad sector on your floppy disk, it just meant that your data was lost.

FT: The floppy disk had a lot of limitations. Did people ask for more data?

FC: They did, there was a whole hacking culture of so-called extended floppy formatting that was huge at that time. We're talking about the late 1980s and the early 1990s. A floppy disk is basically a magnetic disk inside a plastic cover, right? This is read from and written on with a magnetic head. You could compare this to a machine that presses vinyl records. This device doesn't only play records, but it also has a needle to write on them. Now, imagine if this machine did not fully stick to the standardisation of an LP record, but also wrote onto the inside circle, where the label is. In that way you extend the capacity and playback time that is officially available. That's what most programmers did with extended formatting. They wrote code to directly control the magnetic write head and move it to parts of the floppy disk's magnetic surface that were not supposed to be written on. This also meant that you were running into even bigger risks of losing data.

FT: It sounds like people tried to stretch the capabilities of the floppy disk from the moment it arrived. Were there no alternatives on the market that provided more data out of the box?

FC: There were. Sometime later I had a zip drive, which is something like a swappable hard drive that works with cartridges that look like giant size floppy disks. Those had a capacity of around 100 MB, which was huge in comparison to floppy disks. The company that produced them, Iomega, was very successful with them for a couple of years. But then USB arrived. I think it was a small Israeli computer startup that had the idea of soldering flash memory directly onto a USB controller to make a USB memory stick. At the time flash memory cards for digital cameras and media players already existed, but they couldn't be plugged directly into computers.

4.1 - Florian's Sony Mavica camera collection. This picture was taken with his second Mavica FD91. Photo: Florian Cramer

FT: The floppy disk had been around for a very long time. Was USB the medium that prompted its downfall?

FC: I think that the first computer manufacturer that really brought about the death of the floppy disk in the mainstream was Apple with the iMac in 1998. It was the first mainstream computer without a floppy drive. I remember when the iMac was introduced there was a huge outcry with people asking if this computer was practically usable since it didn't have a floppy disk drive. You have to imagine that at that time, home networks were not common, and Internet access was too slow for anything but very small file transfers. To get data from A to B, from one computer to the other, was a huge problem. You would always use physical media. The floppy disk was the most common and convenient way to do this. It was like the lingua franca between computers. You could take a floppy disk that was formatted and written under Windows and then open it on Macintosh and vice versa. The other thing that Apple did back then, besides killing the floppy drive, was to kill the old connection ports of computers, the legacy interfaces. That was just as significant, because the parallel port for printers, serial ports, mouse, and keyboard ports were all replaced by USB, which had not even been developed by Apple.

FT: Were you ever concerned by this development?

FC: Not really, because I wasn't a Macintosh user. I was already using Linux around that time. Linux was always the operating system that gave you full access to all technologies. Even today you can use proprietary CD-ROM drives with non-standard hardware connections to old Soundblaster cards with Linux. It's a hacker-friendly operating system that takes really great care of supporting both new and old hardware and software standards. In that way you almost never get into a situation where you have to throw away a piece of technology just because the management of your device manufacturer has decided that it has become obsolete and stops supporting it with drivers.

FT: Even though floppy disks have remained quite accessible to you, there was a time when you did not use them much. When did they grab your attention again?

FC: I rediscovered the medium when I moved to the Netherlands in 2006. In January 2009 I was in Nijmegen at a festival on cassette tapes at the artist-run venue Extrapool. Some noise musicians whom I like a lot performed there, such as Peter Zincken/ DJ Stront and Frans de Waard, a pioneer of Dutch experimental cassette music. I had a super cheap video camera with me, one of those first-generation no-name Chinese pseudo-HD cameras that couldn't even focus, but had fixed-focus lenses. Back

then I couldn't afford a better camera. When I looked at the material I filmed at the event I realised that it wouldn't be adequate to release it on a traditional video format. What is the digital equivalent of the cassette tape? The floppy disk, of course. It has the same kind of DIY make-up.

FT: In what sense are they similar?

FC: The important thing about the cassette tape in the DIY culture of the 1980s, which I was a part of, is that it was not merely a home-made and low-cost alternative to releasing vinyl or CDs, but also a read/ write medium. If you got a cassette from somebody and you didn't like it, you could just erase it and record your own music over it. The same is true for floppy disks. They were part of a swapping culture, unlike CD-ROMs, which were the mainstream media for distributing digital content from the 1990s to the earlier 2000s. Around floppy disks, there was a similar kind of exchange and piracy culture as with cassette tapes. Full disclosure: the police once busted me in the early 1990s for swapping illegal commercial software. That was my conversion to Open Source/Free Software. When I realised the similarities between cassette swapping culture and floppy swapping culture, I decided to put out my films on floppy disk.

FT: The floppy disk is not the first medium that comes to mind when you think about video. Were there any commercially available floppy video media in the past?

FC: I can think of two cases where floppy disks were historically used for video recording. The first one is the Video floppy, which was a very short lived and very marginal format used in camcorders, developed by Canon. It was physically incompatible to computer floppy disks. The other exception were the Sony Mavica cameras, which were among the first-generation consumer digital photo cameras produced in the 1990s. Their most clever feature was to record to floppy disks, which promised a better ease of use than the various flash memory card formats used by other digital camera manufacturers at the time, like Compact Flash, SmartMedia, xD and later SD cards. You didn't need a card reader, but could just pop the floppy into your computer to take off the pictures. The later generation Mavicas also had a video recording function, using the MPEG-1 codec. This is the codec which was also used on the video CD, a low-resolution precursor of the DVD. On one floppy disk, the Mavicas could record about 15 seconds of video with sound.

FT: Did you create videos with any of these Sony Mavica cameras?

FC: Yes, after I made my first floppy film at the tape event in Nijmegen, I kept finding them at flea markets for a few euro. I now have a whole collection of them, including the very high end Mavica FD91 with a sta-bilised super zoom lens, the Hasselblad or Arri Alexa of floppy disk cameras. I started to give some of them away and used them in a couple of my workshops. In 2009 I recorded a concert by the Norwegian eight-bit band Next Life at a Rotterdam venue called WORM. There are two really great features in all Mavica cameras. First, their floppy drives run at double speed. They read and write the data twice as fast as a normal computer floppy disk drive. Secondly, they have a built-in floppy disk copy function. The camera has an internal 1.4 MB memory buffer which allows you to make copies of any floppy disk inside the camera, not only those recorded with the camera. For this concert, I had bought a whole package of floppy disks. Once I had recorded my 15 second video, I made copies of the floppy disk on the spot and handed them out to the visitors while the band was still playing. I called it 'Floppy Live Cinema', paying homage to the Live Cinema movement started by Martijn van Boven and others at WORM a couple of years earlier. You can use the Mavica camera as a performative medium and have this immediate social experience of swapping and sharing the floppy disks.

FT: Here you still used the floppy cameras as they were intended. However, later you also started to stretch the possibilities of floppy video by means of compression. How did this come about?

FC: At the time, most of my life happened in the Media Design program at the Piet Zwart Institute and at WORM. The first and second generation of students whom I mentored at Piet Zwart Institute founded the moddr_ lab at WORM, a DIY media space. Moddr_ ran a number of community programs, including a pirate cinema event on the night of the Oscar ceremony. The idea was that people brought BitTorrent files of the Oscar nominated films. I thought, okay, that's a challenge for me. I should try to get all the Oscar nominated films on floppy disks, one film per floppy and at full length, not just a few seconds or a few minutes.

FT: How did you manage to do this?

FC: I ended up using animated GIFs. If you have a GIF with a resolution of seven by three pixel, and a reduced frame rate, something like four frames per second, you can fit an entire feature length film onto a single floppy disk. I did this on this moddr_ film evening; each floppy disk had one of the nominated films on them, including *The Wrestler* and *Slumdog Millionaire*. But actually this was all based on a misunderstanding. I thought that everyone needed to bring the video downloaded via BitTorrent and not just the BitTorrent index file. However, this turned out to be a productive misunderstanding. moddr_ later asked me to participate with my floppy films in their retrospective exhibition in Brussels at iMAL, the center for digital cultures and technology.

FT: What is the legality of these floppy pirate films? Did they get you into trouble?

FC: I actually wanted to get sued by Hollywood! I even created a public website, with the film titles in bold letters and the compressed files freely available for download.

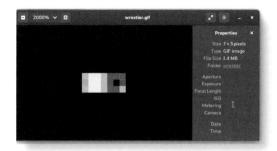

4.2 - A single frame from the Oscar nominated movie '*The Wrestler*, 2008. Source: Florian Cramer

I really put them out in the open. If you used Google to search for the movies, you could easily find the files. Still, I didn't get any legal reaction. Maybe somebody from the studios looked at the floppy films and decided that their seven-by-three pixels were not enough reason to sue me. I was really disappointed!

FT: You later taught people how to do these sorts of compressions themselves. Can you tell us a bit more about your floppy film workshops?

FC: If I remember correctly, the first workshops also happened at moddr_. Back then it was a little more complicated to achieve this kind of compression. It meant that you had to go into the gory details of encoding H.264. This is the most common video codec. It's in almost everything: Blu-ray, most of YouTube and a lot of video streaming. Back then it was still new and not that widespread, but it was the only type of video compression that could fit two or more minutes of video onto a floppy

4.3 - Two stills from Florian's 3.15 minute film *L_TOWERS* (2010), which fits on a single floppy disk in Full HD quality. Source: Florian Cramer

disk in SD resolution. There's a very powerful command line Open Source tool called FFmpeg that uses the x264 codec, which is an Open Source implementation of the H.264 video encoding standard. It's also the software that most streaming services use to transcode uploaded videos. The options that FFmpeg offered were quite esoteric and difficult, so I had to use all kinds of nerdy encoder tweaking parameters to achieve high compression rates. That's what I taught in the workshops.

FT: Is it easier to put films on a floppy disk nowadays?

FC: It's super easy. You now have several simple Open Source graphical tools for video encoding. For example, there is Handbrake, a user-friendly encoder that runs on all operating systems. Back in the day I had to teach people how to use Linux, how to use the command line, how to use FFmpeg's command syntax, and how to use x264's compression optimisation parameters. In

most cases I needed two or three days for a workshop, like at the Transmediale festival in Berlin back in 2012. There I invited the veteran experimental Super 8 filmmaker Dagie Brundert, whom you could call the queen of Super 8. We tried to fuse floppy filmmaking and Super 8 filmmaking. The workshop participants shot Super 8 film, chemically developed the film material in the toilets of the festival, then digitised the material with crude means, and finally put it on floppy disks. If you deal with all these processes and elements, including the materiality and the difficulties of developing film in a public toilet while transferring it to digital video with makeshift means, you encounter many glitches. You experience the same kind of materiality in the analogue and in the so-called digital medium, which – upon closer view – is not actually a digital medium.

FT: Why would you say the floppy disk is not a digital medium?

4.4 - Still from one of Florian's 15 second Sony Mavica recording of the Norwegian band *Next Life* performing at WORM Rotterdam, 2009. Source: Florian Cramer

4.5 - *MR_CMP* - Florian Cramers floppy film adaption of Rosa Menkman's video *Mr. Compression*, 2012. Source: Florian Cramer

FC: Because it is based on magnetic and electronic hardware, and that hardware is always analog. I think my workshop helps you understand that this common idea of digital technology as a virtualisation or dematerialisation is blatantly mistaken, and in most cases, based on a lack of actually understanding the technology. By doing these workshops, the intrinsic material qualities of the particular medium are really in your face and you understand how it is structured. With analogue film you can see the grain and you can see the chemicals. It's the same with digital technology. If you go down to the level of highly compressed data on a floppy disk, you can see all the artifacts and the technical workings of that medium. It helps to demystify the technology and forms the necessary groundwork for understanding it in its larger economic, ecological, and political dimensions. In that sense, my floppy filmmaking project is much indebted to the spirit of early 1970s structural filmmaking. The floppy disk is a wonderful example of a

medium that complicates our notion of what we define as analogue and digital, as well as what we see as 'old media' and 'new media'.

FT: What other virtues does the floppy disk have?

FC: Well, I also find the aspect of constraint really important. That has to do with my own background. As a scholar in Comparative Literature, I wrote my PhD thesis on combinatorial poetics, from poetic Lullism in the Renaissance to the present. One of the most significant groups in this field is the French Oulipo, which I studied extensively. It was founded in 1961 by among others Raymond Queneau, a former surrealist, who was later joined by mathematicians like François Le Lionnais. The novelist Italo Calvino became a member, too. Georges Perec was maybe the most consequent and radical of all Oulipo writers. The poetics of Oulipo are based on very playful and ironic applications of mathematics and computation to literary

4.6 - Florian's film CORARIA (Cora Schmeiser performing John Cage's 'Aria'), 2009. Source: Florian Cramer

writing. I think they are so much more clever and better than other approaches to computational arts, because they didn't buy into any positivist or new technology hype. They always treated computation in a pataphysical manner. The Oulipo poetics are based on the principle of constraint. An outstanding example of this is Georges Perec's 300 page novel *A Void* that doesn't have a single occurrence of the letter 'e'. This is difficult to do as a writer, but also results in something more interesting than writing the same book conventionally.

FT: In what sense is using the floppy disk today such a constraint?

FC: The constraint of the floppy is not just its limited storage capacity. If that were the only criterion, you could also build a USB stick with only 1.4 MB. There is also its transmission speed. It is a very slow medium. If you play audio and video straight from a floppy disk, often the pure hardware transmission rate of the disk data is too slow for real-time playback, so you get stutters, breaks, glitches,

buffer problems, and even buffer break-downs. A third constraint is the unreliability of the medium. Unlike with hard disk drives, which use essentially the same electromagnetic technology as floppy disks, only much improved, there's no internal checksumming of the data to automatically 'repair' damaged files, and the magnetic surface of the floppy disk is not vacuum-sealed, but fully exposed. It's easy for only a piece of dust to get in, land on the magnetic surface, and destroy data. These constraints are interesting to work with. This also operates against the colonialist techno-utopian idea of new technology as a search for the new frontier, an infinite expansion into new and even bigger territories. This is a very wasteful and questionable approach to computing, similar to how average cars have grown from compact cars to SUVs. I'm not saying that using floppy disks is ecologically responsible, but thinking of how to do things with limited means can have interesting results. It requires you to think more broadly about what you're doing.

FT: As you've hit upon the topic of ecology, this might be a good point to talk about the future of the floppy. Do you think there is a role for floppy disks in the coming years?

FC: Well, I have no idea what the actual ecological footprint of the floppy disk is, so I would strongly refrain from any statements regarding its sustainability. USB sticks must be much more ecologically reasonable, because one stick uses less plastic and metal than a single floppy disk, while its capacity is several thousand times larger, and they last longer on top of that. Concerning the question of whether or not the floppy has a bright future, I would say it depends. For me, it's not a means to an end. The floppy disk is a tool, a device, but not in a completely utilitarian way. It has become an experimental device that I more or less accidentally started using for a filmmaking project. It turned out to be an interesting challenge to work with the device, but I'm not ideologically or romantically glued to it. Flipbooks or receipt printers are also interesting for artistic experimentation. Whether or not I continue working with floppy disks depends on whether there are enough interesting opportunities or necessities to do so. I do have a number of floppy films that are still unreleased, though.

FT: Are you concerned with the preservation of your floppy films? Do you think that they should be archived?

FC: I think it's for other people to decide if they are valuable enough. However, it's very easy to preserve the data of a floppy disk. You can just make a disk image and start your own archive. I would encourage more use of USB sticks. I think they're now on the way to becoming endangered in the same way that floppy disks are. The industry wants you to use the so-called cloud. Many people don't have personal computers anymore, but only use mobile phones. This often makes it impossible or difficult to transfer data from and to USB sticks. Still, USB sticks are one of the few media that people can freely share with no outside interference and control. In hacker terminology, you call that a Sneakernet. A Sneakernet isn't made up of cables or wireless transmissions, but of people in their sneakers, their shoes, walking from A to B to copy data between computers and other devices, completely bypassing electronic networks like the Internet. The floppy disk is also a Sneakernet technology. That was really what it had been invented for. At the time other forms of networking were not widely available. I think it would be very interesting to look into Sneakernets and their potential on a much larger scale.

'Just enjoy everything while it's there, especially this retro stuff, because it's not going to last forever.'

LOOKING FORWARD BY LOOKING BACK

CLINT BASINGER (US) is the driving force behind the Lazy Game Reviews (LGR) YouTube channel, providing weekly coverage of retro tech, classic computer gaming, oddware, thrifting tech tales, and more. Besides regularly creating videos on obscure and redundant forms of disk-based media, Basinger is also a collector of big box floppy disk games.

We talked with Clint about what it means to create content about obsolete technology and what role YouTube plays in shaping the community around it. Is the floppy disk the ignition key to retro computing?

Floppy Totaal (FT): Hi Clint, glad we could meet today. Let's start with some very basic questions that are sometimes difficult to answer. Who are you and what do you do?

Clint Basinger (CB): Well, my name is Clint Basinger, and I run a YouTube channel called LGR. I guess I am a content creator, whatever that means. I've been doing that for over a decade now. LGR began life as a sort of variety channel, covering whatever topics came to mind, but it evolved into a very retro tech focused, modern look at nostalgia. I sometimes describe it as looking forward by looking back. So, giving context to where we are now, by looking back at where we've come from.

FT: How did your channel come to be?

CB: It was initially just a hobby that I did in my spare time. I kind of hated my job and just wanted to do anything else. I've always wanted to do creative work. It wasn't until around seven or eight years ago that the channel started to become a moneymaking thing. This happened pretty much by accident. I was just having a good time, messing around with old computers, reconnecting with things from my childhood and teenage years; things that I either remembered having or completely missed out on.

FT: So you were already into old tech before you started creating content about it on YouTube?

CB: Yes, for a number of years I was doing random computer repairs as a side job. I would go to local thrift stores, businesses, or people's homes and they would be like: 'Oh, I've got this old computer that's sitting in the basement. Do you want it?' So I would take it home and fix it up and either resell it, or just mess around with it myself. That was really how I got back into the computers that I remembered as a kid. Before 2003 or 2004 I actually didn't have much interest in retro stuff at all; it still seemed too recent. As the years went on, I grew more of an appreciation for all the things I accumulated doing computer repairs.

FT: Sounds like you were pretty busy, even back then. So where does the name Lazy Game Reviews come from? Are you really that lazy?

CB: Guess not anymore. As it started, the videos were meant to be very lazy. There would be no script, very little editing, and not really any thought put into it. It was a personal challenge for me to put out one video every week, just to get my mind off of other things. I've been doing one video a week ever since. So yes, it was meant to be lazy, but it turned into something not so lazy.

FT: You are quite outspoken about your enthusiasm for floppy disks. If I remember correctly, you used to have an introduction to your YouTube channel that presented the floppy

disk as the key to your channel. What does the medium mean to you?

CB: The floppy disk for me was always a symbol of everything old school in terms of computing. It's an icon. You just always see it, whether it's as a save icon in a program or when a character is using something old in a movie. It's a symbol of the antiquated, even though it was used up until as recently as 20 years ago. So yeah, the floppy functioned almost as an ignition key starts up a car, but instead it started up a video.

FT: Do you have a personal history with floppy disks? Do you remember when you first started using them?

CB: Yes, in fact, one of my very earliest memories was using a floppy disk. It was a 5.25-inch; a single sided floppy disk, I think, on an Apple IIe. I couldn't have been more than four or five years old. It was at a computer lab at school – my very first school and the very first computer I ever saw. The teacher handed each of us our own floppy disk in class. We got one to use for the entire year. I had no idea what any of that meant. I didn't even know what a computer was. But as soon as she showed us that you could save something on the disk and retrieve it the next day, that's when something clicked in my mind. This was something I wanted to do everything with. I wanted to figure out all there was to know about computers.

FT: Have you used floppy disks ever since? Or was there a period when they were less prevalent in your life?

CB: Yes, as soon as I got a CD ROM drive it felt like I was done with them. I never actually messed with zipdisks or anything like that. I pretty much went straight from floppies to USB. For a while I felt that I would never need to use one again, especially when rewritable CDs came along. It was when I started repairing old computers and I needed a boot disk that I figured I might as well use a floppy. Using them again came about more as a necessity. It was not a joy until much later, once I started to appreciate them retroactively.

FT: This appreciation has grown into quite a big collection of floppy disks. What does it look like at the moment?

CB: Oh dear ... in terms of sheer numbers I probably have over 5 000 big box games. Each one of them is special to me; almost all of them I never owned or was unable to afford as a kid. I remember going into game stores and being in awe of all the walls of boxes, and now I have walls of boxes myself. With the games came the hardware to get them all running. Almost every game needs something individual, like a video card, sound card, certain speed of CPU, an amount of RAM and so on. I had to start building computers to get certain games running. It seemed like every time that I thought I had one that could run most things, something else came

CLINT BASINGER

5.1 - Clint Basinger in his home studio, where he creates most of his video content. Photo: Clint Basinger

along and I had to build another one. At this point, I don't know how many hundreds of computers I have. Since doing LGR people from all around the world send in stuff every week. Something I've never shown on video is that there are multiple rooms at my storage facility that are full of the most random stuff you've ever seen – computer parts, games, software, cables, and weird little peripherals. It's kind of gotten out of hand to be honest.

FT: You still use a lot of floppy disks in your videos. Do you always boot programs and games directly from floppy disks?

CB: Sure, I use them just about every day now. It is kind of my job to keep these computers going and do videos on them. It's not always the most convenient option, but it's certainly the one that is the most supported by almost every one of these computers that I use. I've gone out of my way to keep that going by using USB floppy drives or making sure that if I get a more modern computer, it has a floppy drive header. That way I can put an old drive in a new machine and very easily transfer things. I keep a number of computers just for transferring files. One is connected to the Internet, but it's got four or five floppy drives in there of various capacities and formats. It's often just the quickest, easiest way to get something working for a video.

FT: That's a very practical approach to the medium. Wouldn't emulation be even more practical?

CB: Well, anytime that I want to install a game or get a version of DOS or Windows going, I prefer using the original disks instead of floppy emulators. I've used them; it's fine and it's convenient. But there's also something oddly inconvenient about them, because I can't see the individual disks. You have to format things to get them onto a USB stick, just to make sure that they line up as virtual disks. Sometimes it's just easier to have an actual box of floppies, providing they still work.

FT: Let's talk a little bit about YouTube. You primarily create content for this platform. I was wondering, what are the biggest challenges in using YouTube?

CB: YouTube is constantly changing, to the point where I don't really know if I'm keeping up with it all the time. In fact, I often feel like I'm chasing my own tail, trying to figure out what the algorithm is doing this week, or what new changes happen in terms of content, ID matches, and copyrights. There's always something. But even with that out of the way, there's just the personal challenge of trying to make sure that my content doesn't get stale. Growing stale is probably the biggest crime on YouTube, other than doing something controversial. That's probably the thing that I'm most worried about – just coming up with ideas that are similar enough to what I've already done, but different enough to bring in new eyes and keep people interested. Doing that every week is increasingly hard to achieve, especially in the retro world. I'm going into newer and newer things. Instead of just covering the 80s era I have moved to the late 90s and even the mid 2000s. Windows XP is also becoming nostalgic somehow.

FT: What are the positives about being on YouTube?

CB: For me, it's the community; the back and forth with people, discovering other folks that are into the same things as me, and sharing what I enjoy. All of a sudden other people want to see me having fun with the stuff that I would be doing in my own free time. There's really no other platform that allows me to do that in this way. Before YouTube, I was on forums all the time talking with people just through text. This filled a need, but once YouTube came along, it replaced it for me.

FT: It seems like there has been quite a shift over the years in the content you create. Your videos have become more and more tech-oriented, while game reviews have taken a backseat. How did this come to be?

CB: This change wasn't really something that I noticed while it was happening. The more I used old computers, the more I realised that the way I was using them wasn't necessarily very interesting anymore. I figured that there was so much more I could do with a computer besides covering games. Anybody could play them on modern hardware by just download-ing an emulator like DOSBox or something. For me, the hardware side of it is something that you can't emulate. The actual hands-on experience became more special than cover-ing another DOS game that literally anybody could do. In a way, emulation ruined the experience. When you have everything avail-able to you, there's nothing available to you. I latched on to the hardware side of things and the more I did this, the more I realised that there was a lot of content there that I had not thought about covering before. For instance, I always took for granted the way that sound and video cards work or how upgrades to different file formats and operating systems operated. I never really thought about these sorts of things until I started messing around with them again and showing them in videos. The response was much more intense than it was when I was just covering videogames.

FT: Did you reach a different audience after this change?

CB: It was certainly a bigger audience, or perhaps a more engaged audience. People started providing their own feedback. A lot of times stuff goes wrong in my video, so things are always up for debate. People are like: 'Oh, did you try this? Oh, I was a technician. I had this problem. I remember this thing. Oh, here's this website. I wrote this driver or piece of software here. Try this on the next one'. Every video builds up to the next one. It's now a mountain of stuff that started as a molehill. With games, it's kind of one-sided, while with hardware, I feel it's more collabo-rative. There's a community that's constantly involved in tweaking and creating things, and that engages more with the videos as a result.

FT: Does this involvement of a larger community also influence your choice of certain video topics?

CB: It does. I always begin with whatever I'm interested in on a given week, but if that doesn't really match up with something that I think the community is going to latch on to, I try to change direction. Still, I've also put out plenty of videos that I thought wouldn't do well … and they didn't do well, but at least I had fun with them. On the other hand, there have been videos that I thought would do well, and they didn't. Actually, it's videos that I don't think will do so great that end up doing well. That's been the surprise in recent years.

FT: Can you give an example of one of these surprise hits?

CB: There was the *Doom on a Calculator* video. That was meant to be just a throwaway thing. I did it in an afternoon when I needed a video out for that week. I just wanted something done quickly, but I think that it's my number one video now. I also did a video about the turbo button on the computer cases from back in the day. Why are they there? Or the key locks on the front of computers. That's one of those things I always took for granted. I thought everybody knew what that was, but then I ended up getting a couple of million views. I still don't understand exactly why that took off, but for some reason it struck a nerve.

FT: It seems that these three examples function as introductions to a pretty particular topic. They're almost educational. Do you see your channel as a sort of entry point into the tech world?

CB: Every so often I do get emails from parents or kids who tell me that they got into vintage computers because of me. I actually heard from a kid not too long ago who said that he started watching my videos in middle school and now he's going to college to study computer science. He says he would not have done so if he hadn't watched my videos. That's always cool to see, but I don't really know how much of that I can take credit for. Maybe these people would have soaked it in anyway, just through cultural osmosis. There's a broader interest for retro things going around in general media right now, like TV and movies and all that. Perhaps this also makes people seek out my videos.

FT: Do you think the growing interest in retro tech relates directly to nostalgia?

CB: I think nostalgia is a tricky thing. It's hard to define from person to person, because some people have nostalgia for good things and some people have it for bad things. In a way, I have more nostalgia for all of the tech memories where things went wrong, floppy disks in particular, because they were constantly not working. There was something interesting about that. When something did work, it was very, very special. I remember when I shared a floppy

5.2 – Even modern smart phones can use a floppy disk drive, as LGR demonstrates in the 2018 video *LGR - Using a Floppy Disk Drive on a Smartphone*. Source: YouTube

with a friend or got one for Christmas, I would hope and pray that it would work while installing it. What I'm buying into is recreating just a little bit of that unique feeling of when things finally did go right.

FT: We live in a time where a lot of physical media is disappearing. It seems that flash memory is already on its way out. Do you think that there will ever be another medium like the floppy disk that will evoke the same sort of nostalgia or emotional attachment?

CB: It's hard to imagine that somebody would be nostalgic for anything from the current time. There's kind of a cutoff in my mind when things went solid state. Like, that stuff doesn't seem real to me in the way that even spinning hard disks do. There's been an interesting trend in the past couple of years where people seem to have a very high amount of nostalgia for hard disk based iPods. I never thought that would be a thing, since it was just a throwaway device that only got better. Still, there are some YouTube channels that only cover hard disk iPods and they have just exploded. I think that there's something about spinning magnetic media; they feel like they could break down at any time. Something that always surprised me is that whenever I show a hard disk in one of my videos, or you can hear one clicking and running away in the background, people comment that they've missed that sound. Computers are silent now. So yeah, maybe people will feel nostalgic about hard disk media. Perhaps optical media will get there eventually, but it doesn't seem like my generation cares.

FT: Is it viable to make money from obsolete technology?

CB: It can be. I know of a guy and all he does for a living is find old computer parts and sells them through eBay. He doesn't even clean them up. He just puts them out there. He happens to have a number of sources, because he used to work at Microsoft or some other big company. He makes a living from both selling and repurposing stuff, especially keyboards. Another thing I never saw coming is the keyboard collectors. They're insane. They will pay $1 000 for the little basic keyboard that you thought was worthless five or ten years ago, with a certain type of key capper or spring mechanism. Either they just want to use the keyboards themselves or they break them down into parts and sell the individual components to make new ones. So yes, if you're in the right part of the retro market, there's a lot of money to be made.

FT: You did some videos in which you combine old and new technology. For example, you made a video in which you attach a floppy disk reader to your phone. Why did you want to do this? Did you find this hack useful after making the video?

CB: The video was made very much for fun, but I did try the same trick on a couple of other devices. I wanted to see if it worked on a Raspberry Pi, because I was going to do a video about a 3d printed IBM PC with a Raspberry Pi and hook an actual floppy drive up to it. It did work, but the project never went anywhere. It lost a little bit of the magic for me when I realised that it doesn't actually read or write from the disk in the same way that it does on an old computer. It creates an image of the disk as soon as you insert it, so the whole thing is just there sitting in memory. It's not doing anything to the disk itself, like writing back to it. Still, I'm always looking around, or sort of hoping for new USB floppy devices, just for ease of archiving and backup.

FT: The thing that strikes me with these sorts of hardware hacks is that they're usually a solution to a question that nobody asked for. Even though you can boot floppy disks on a phone or play *DOOM* on a calculator, not a lot of people are very likely to do so. What is the appeal of these sorts of projects? It doesn't seem very practical?

CB: No, it's not, but I find that when using anything that is obsolete or old the entire point is that it is impractical. It's the nerdy engineer type challenge that gets people into the hobby. They want to see if they can do something, just because they can. Maybe somebody hasn't tried it at all, or if they have tried it, it hasn't really been documented very well. I always, for instance, knew that you could put a floppy drive on a phone but I had never tried it until I made that video. I also find the idea of legacy support very fascinating. Just seeing how old you can go with how new you can go, and sort of finding something in between. It's kind of like supercharging an old car, or making a new car run very badly.

5.3 – A view of Clint's collection of 'boxed' video games, many of them on floppy disks. Photo: Clint Basinger

FT: There's something very symbolic about that, right? To most people, technology is first and foremost a practical component in their lives. It's quite interesting to do something that goes completely against this idea. I wonder, are you optimistic about the future of technology?

CB: Well, I'm excited about it, but I'm not sure if I want to fully embrace it. There are a lot of things that I would miss. When it comes to games and software I do prefer that there's a physical release of something, just so I don't have the feeling that they're just on loan to me from a giant corporation. Unfortunately, these releases often end up being overly priced cash grabs, and not just the norm like they used to be. I think there is something that got lost there. For me it just doesn't feel right if all I have is a bunch of files, and they can be on any computer. If I have my entire game collection accessible through the cloud on my phone I will never access it. But if you sat me down behind one computer with one floppy drive and one system, I'll mess around with things all afternoon, simply because it feels like a challenge to get each game running. There's just something fun and enjoyable there that I don't see coming back in a mainstream way with modern tech. It's all moving towards convenience over everything else.

FT: What do you have lined up for the future?

CB: Just more of the same; lots of old computers, lots of old games. For the end of this year I'm working on a couple of Christmas videos. I don't really plan very far ahead. A couple of weeks at a time is about all I can manage. At the moment I try to track down the things that are slowly going away so I can get them on the Internet and make a video about them before I can't find them anymore. I receive a lot of things in the mail now that I can only borrow and not keep. That's fine, because I only have so much storage space, but it is another interesting side effect of all these collectors popping up over the past few years. People used to send stuff over to me and say: 'Keep it, I don't care, I don't need it.' Now they want it back, because it has become too valuable.

FT: One final question: where do you think floppy disks are heading?

CB: Ah well, sadly, floppy disks are all going away. That's just sort of the deterioration process. I don't really know where they're going except to the landfill probably. Of course, it depends on the quality of the disks, but they're degrading and falling apart like everything else. That's something you can take away from anything: an appreciation of what we have now. Just enjoy everything while it's here, especially this retro stuff, because it's not going to last forever. Take it day by day, remember where you came from, where you're going, and don't forget to live right now. It's not going to last.

'As we go forward, things become more generic, more minimal and more functional. Some of the charm and uniqueness is taken away.'

EVERYONE, EVERYTHING SHAPES US

NICK GENTRY (UK) is a London based artist who repurposes obsolete media as the raw material for his artwork. Besides computer punch cards and VHS tapes, he makes use of floppy diskettes, donated to him by people from all over the world. The disks function as the canvas for his oil paintings, which are influenced by the development of consumerism, technology, identity, and cyberculture in society.

We interviewed Nick in the midst of the COVID-19 pandemic, a time when he, like so many others, was bound to his home studio. What role do floppy disks play in shaping our collective identity? How can this be mediated through portrait painting?

Floppy Totaal (FT): Hello Nick, how are things over there at the moment?

Nick Gentry (NG): Very good. I've been able to carry on working from the studio in my garden. We've just had a baby, who is now six months old. There's plenty to keep me busy right now. I'm very lucky!

FT: We would like to talk to you about floppy disks, a medium you are quite familiar with. Do you feel comfortable being labelled as a floppy disk artist?

NG: I'm okay with that. I used to think that I didn't want to be pigeonholed as a certain type of artist, but at the end of the day, if people want to say what I am, that's fine. After all, there have been floppy disks throughout my life and I've had a good experience with them. So yeah, why not?

FT: You also repurpose other kinds of media in your artwork, right?

NG: Yes, I'm interested in a lot of obsolete media, like film negatives, VHS tapes, and computer punch cards. Some of these were around during my childhood, but I also like to think beyond my own life and focus on what came before it. Computing and data are interesting to me culturally. Through punch cards I want to explore these topics further. They have a different aesthetic, a different feel, and a different level of data storage. Yet, they are no less culturally significant than the floppy disk.

FT: When did floppy disks start popping up in your life? Can you remember when you decided to use them in your art?

NG: I think the first time I used a floppy disk was in my childhood at a very young age. I have a lot of memories of my brother and I playing games on a Commodore Amiga. The moment I started using them in my art is less clear. I remember messing around with them in the studio. I didn't have much of a concept when I started working with floppy disks, but through conversations I began to see that there might be something going on with the medium that would be worth investigating. I've always been interested in identity and the question of what defines it. Is this something singular or collective? A person can't exist on their own. Everyone they meet, including their friends and family, shape them. There's always an exchange going on. I thought about that for a while and figured that a large part of this happens digitally now. What are the origins of this? That's the cool part about it – it's not just about a material exchange, it's about the cultural side as well.

FT: Wherever there is culture and memory, nostalgia lurks. Do you think people might approach your work nostalgically?

NG: I'm sure some people that yearn to live in the 1990s do, but that's not the way I see it. It's not a nostalgia trip for me, even if I did enjoy that era. I'm quite happy with the present day and curious about what might happen in the future. I see floppy disks as cultural artifacts that remind us of who we are and where we are going. They might look humble and fun, but they actually stand for so much more. There is a lot to engage with.

FT: What makes the floppy disk such an engaging medium?

NG: Well, first of all, it's the colour and the shape. Floppy disks are small. You can hold them in your hand, making them easier to identify with on a personal level. Maybe it's the blend of plastic and metal on paper, combined into one unit. The floppy disk is very unique in that way. As we go forward, things become more generic, more minimal and more functional. Some of the charm and uniqueness is taken away. There is also something appealing about the fact that they're so limited, only 1.44 MB of data on a single disk. The small scale makes it easier to engage with as a human. Anything vast and open, like a supermarket, doesn't feel that personal. Just think about a small, cosy cafe; there's something nice about confinement. You can experience the total area. The bigger we go, the less compatible it becomes with our brains. Because of current technology we now need to find ways to compartmentalise our lives. That's where floppy disks come in.

FT: You have been using disks in your artwork for quite some time. Can you give us a short description of the process behind your floppy disk portraits?

NG: Sure, though there's no beginning or end to it necessarily. People might see my work in the gallery and decide that they want to take part in the process, so they send me disks. I take those into the studio, where I sort them according to colour and store them in various drawers. After that I assemble the disks into a portrait; it's like putting them down into a mosaic. Once this is done, I paint a portrait on them using oil paint. I do this in a quite traditional painting style, but the main aspect is the collage of the materials. Finally, it's important to get the work out there for people to see. I put them on social media, or in a gallery. I want people to see what I'm doing and to take part in it.

FT: I noticed that you also sell digital copies of your artworks on your website. Is this the ideal way to share your work today?

NG: Well, an original painting on the wall will always be preferable to me. I do like the tactile nature of things, but I offer my work in both ways now. To me it makes sense to offer a high-res download if someone wants one. It helps to connect with people through my work. They can do whatever they want with their download, except for commercial uses.

FT: In what other ways have you shared your work?

NG: About ten years ago, I was messing about in the studio with stencils and things like that. My work was not shown in galleries at the time, so I used to leave artworks around the streets of London for people to pick up. This helped me to carry on with what I was doing. When people took them home it showed me that my art wasn't just some weird project that nobody could connect with. I feel like artists have to do something that's relevant, like talking about the moment that we're in and the technology of the time. Still, it's very hard to make an artwork about what is going on while it is still happening. It helps to look at things in retrospect. This gives you the time to build an idea around it, rather than just a knee jerk reaction.

FT: One of the ways this social interaction comes back in your work is through the floppy disks that people donate to you. Is this the main source for your material?

NG: Yes, the disks come from lots of different people and from as many different countries. They send them to me in boxes with little handwritten letters that tell me the stories behind the material. I also ask people to donate disks if they have them lying around. Sometimes they're very happy to do so, but at other times, they still have a personal link with the objects and they don't want to lose them. Even though the disks are completely obsolete and they cannot use them physically, they still want to retain them as a memento of the past. It's quite important to me that people take part in what I do, because a reflection of their history is shown within my work. These works are not about any specific individual, but a sort of patchwork. Seeing all these different floppy disks together, which come from so many different places, is a way of sharing experiences.

FT: Did you ever embed any of your own data, or floppy disks, into your art?

NG: I think I did early on. My mum gave me some disks from my locker in the loft. I didn't have that many left. There are, however, also some commonalities. When looking through a box of disks I have received, there are so many games and titles familiar to me. It's a shared history in that respect. It sometimes makes me wonder how many floppy disks have been made, what happened to them, and where they are now. They were so personal to everyone and now the vast majority of them are lying somewhere in a landfill.

FT: It sounds like you are also concerned with the data that's on the disks. Do you ever boot them up to see what's on there?

NG: I must have received thousands of disks, but I've never looked into one. I don't have the means. If I did, I probably would do so. Still, I find looking at the labels quite interesting, as they give you a clue to what's on the disk. With the first few portraits I made I would paint over the labels and only kept the form of the disks. However, the more of them I received in the studio, the more I realised the most interesting part about them are the handwritten notes, the clues as to what the data might be. I decided to keep them intact and show more of their raw material.

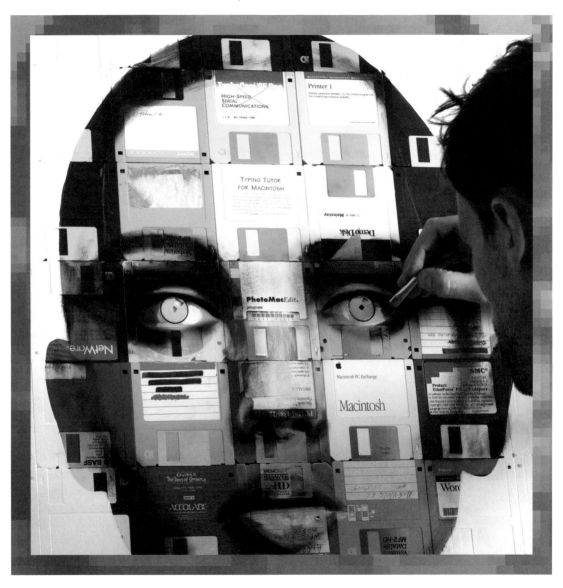

6.1 - Nick painting one of his floppy disk portraits. Photo: Nick Gentry

FT: Would you allow people to pull data from the floppies that are part of your artworks?

NG: Sure, I don't know how you would do it, though. It feels like I've locked them down. Someone would really have to dislike the painting and take it apart first. But you know, it's an interesting thing, one or two of these disks must have some interesting or valuable data on them.

FT: Let's talk about portraiture. You are very invested in this form. What's the particular appeal of the portrait for you?

NG: Well, I've always loved drawing faces, so portraiture seemed like the way to go. Portraiture feels like one of the art forms that are currently disappearing, but I couldn't think of a more interesting time for portraiture. If you think of our faces, you are also considering their biometric data and so on. Faces are being changed more than ever, for instance, through plastic surgery and online photo filters. You can change your actual appearance, but you can also have an avatar to represent your face. These tend to be in our own image, but different: better looking for instance. For me these aspects are a big part of the appeal of portrait painting today.

FT: I wonder, who are the people that you paint? Is there a connection between who is being portrayed and the data that is on the floppy disks?

NG: At the start there was obviously a temptation to portray Steve Jobs or some other well-known figure in the world of data. I did create a portrait of Tim Berners-Lee once, but it didn't feel right. It wasn't in keeping with the ethos of the project, which is about the collective. I could of course also have painted a portrait of someone that sent me his or her disks, but again, it's not about the individual. I decided to create anonymous figures of human forms. I wouldn't even say people, because they do not portray anyone in particular. In that way the work stays focused on the collective.

FT: This year you organised a social art project in collaboration with the National Health Service. The project was connected to the COVID-19 pandemic and focussed on particular individuals. Could you tell us a little more about this venture and the artwork that came out of it?

NG: Sure. I felt I had to do something to be a part of what was happening, rather than just being a spectator. I wanted to use my art in a positive way and so decided to paint portraits of NHS workers in the UK. I invited them to send me their selfies, and I re-created them with computer punch cards. When I started working with them, I didn't know much about the medium yet, but I was still drawn to them. After a while it started to make sense. There's a lot of data going around in a global pandemic, it's actually at the heart of it. We track where people are going for instance.

6.2 – A future work in progress. Photo: Nick Gentry

Punch cards were used for finding data about people and storing that data. I thought it made sense to use them for these portraits.

FT: A lot of our data nowadays isn't stored on a physical medium, but out of reach, in the so-called cloud. How do you feel about recent technological developments and the disappearance of data carriers that coincides with this?

NG: I'm generally a very optimistic person, but I find some things scary. I think that the optimistic way to engage with something is to talk about it. A negative approach is pretending everything is just okay and ignoring things that then become problems later on. It's fine to have issues and concerns and worries, and great to talk about them. That's why floppy disks are important. They offer us a chance to talk about where we come from, our roots. We need to know who we are to be able to figure out where we want to go. Technology can be very exciting and have many benefits, but it's very easy to get lost when dealing with it. There are so many options now, but we don't have much time to spare. We need to use it wisely.

FT: It seems there is currently so much going on that we, as humans, have trouble keeping up. Do you feel we are reaching some sort of historical tipping point?

NG: Yes, it does feel like we're living in a very specific moment for humanity. When you take a look at the environment, it's obviously suffering. There's no question about that. We need to go back in human history to know the real price of what we've developed. I'm not against technology, but there's a huge amount of technological waste that is more or less out of sight and out of mind. I try to live in a way that's not too bad for the planet, but it's obvious we're leaving an impact. In my lifetime there has been close to a doubling of the global population, which is an incredible amount of change to deal with. It makes sense that we have to change the way we live. I think that young people are more aware of this now.

FT: How do you think people 30 years from now will look at your art? I can imagine that they will not have had direct contact with floppy disks like we did. How will people that don't know what a floppy disk is perceive your work?

NG: I do often think about that when I'm creating a piece. I wonder how it will look to someone 100 years in the future. How would it look to an alien just landed here on earth? What would they understand about humanity? I think that helps to create art really, when you test it out and take the perspective from someone way in the future. I've had a lot of contact with people that are younger than me, like students, and they don't know what floppy disks are. To them it's an artefact that you'd see in a museum. I think it wouldn't be that bad if they ended up there, because they are a key part of how our lives were organised and they played a

6.3 - Profile Number 18, oil paint & used computer disks on wood, 85cm x 81cm, 2019.
Source: Nick Gentry / Licensed by DACS/Artimage, London

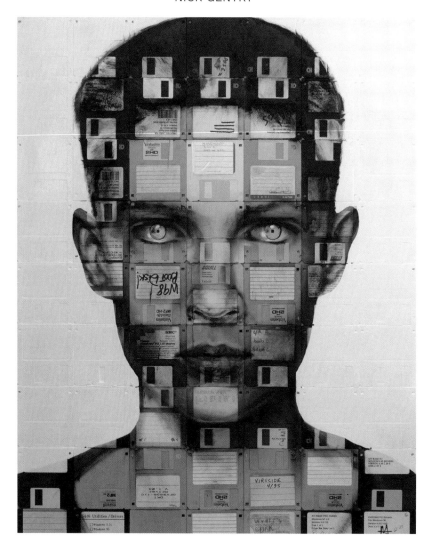

6.4 – Virucide, oil paint & used computer disks on wood, 85cm x 63cm, 2012.
Source: Nick Gentry / Licensed by DACS/Artimage, London

big part in the digital revolution. Through my art I'm trying to create something that gives you a visual sense of who we are and what we have been doing for the last few decades.

FT: Our lives are currently also being shaped by media other than the floppy disk. Would you consider using these in your artwork in future?

NG: Well, I have to move through things in order to build them into what I'm doing. I usually take a very long time. It took me 20 years to figure out how to use floppy disks. It's such an unpredictable future right now that I think it's impossible to speculate. I'm interested in AI and machine learning, though.

FT: What do you think the future holds for the floppy disk? Is there a future for the medium?

NG: It is still the icon for saving things, so for now it's hanging in there. Hopefully, it will keep playing its role as a reminder of this unique moment in time. Before the floppy disk, the world was so different. I think you can point to the floppy disk as something that was at the centre of everything changing. As an object, I think that it should be remembered in that way. I'm sure that floppy disks are in some museums right now, but I don't think they are being given enough consideration. There's a bigger conversation to be had around the medium. So yes, there is a future for the floppy disk, but probably not functionally. Besides tiling the walls perhaps...

'Great creative work often happens not because of complete freedom, but due to limitations. Limitations mean that you have to think outside of the box.'

A MEMORABLE SORT OF LIMITATION

FOONE TURING (US) is a media collector, hardware hacker, and Twitter personality. They curated an award-winning exhibit on floppy disks at the Computer History Museum in Mountain View, built a series of impractical keyboards, and crafted the (formerly Sierra) Death Generator, a tool for making fake video game dialogue screenshots.

At the end of 2020 we discussed the comings and goings of running a retro tech Twitter profile and the appeal of creating the ultimate crappy keyboard. Is the floppy disk perhaps the perfect creative bottleneck?

FT: Hi Foone, how are you? Any hopes and wishes for the New Year?

FoT: Hello there, I just hope 2021 will be better than 2020. I'm looking forward to a lot of stuff. I have five different DOS projects I was hoping to finish up before December, but I don't think any of them are going to be done in time. They're all missing one part or another, so I've had some anxiety that the year is about to end. I'm excited and in anguish!

FT: We're very happy to talk to you today, because you have quite a reputation. I'm not sure if you are aware of this, but some people have referred to you as the floppy disk king of Twitter. Do you have an idea where this comes from?

FoT: Probably from me being the one that has the most followers on Twitter of anyone that posts about floppies. Plus, I've had my icon set as a floppy pretty much the entire time I've been on there. It's gotten to the point where if anything happens with floppy disks, I get people mentioning me for the next week, even if I already posted about it. I remember a year or so ago an astronaut found some floppy disks on the International Space Station in a locker somewhere. Apparently, they had been there since the very first mission. For at least the next month, everyone was asking me if I had seen this. Just the other day, someone put the film *Shrek* on a floppy, and of course, people keep sending me that.

It's amusing, even if I'm not out there doing anything with floppies, people will tell me about floppy stuff. I Retweet it, which only enhances my persona as 'the floppy person'.

FT: Do people ever refer you back to your own projects, because they weren't aware that you were involved?

FoT: Yes, that definitely happened, but not with floppy disks specifically. I put *Doom* on a pregnancy test once. People said that that was nothing, because they saw somebody put *Skyrim* on the same device. Well, that was me, right before I put *Doom* on it. A lot of the times I do something it gets reposted to Reddit and such, and the attribution goes away. I only post my things on Twitter, so it's just a little video and there's my name next to it. Someone might take that video and put it on Reddit, the attribution gets lost and then people start sending me that link.

FT: Are you bothered with that lack of recognition?

FoT: Not really. From the things I've had go viral, I know that it's usually a good thing. It just means more people are seeing it. If I was a YouTuber making money off of this, I might be more bothered, but this isn't my main job, even though I have a Ko-Fi and Patreon account.

FT: Can you tell us a little more about your background? What is your main job? Are there a lot of floppies involved?

FoT: I'm a computer programmer, kind of in the DevOps area. I do continuous integration stuff, so testing systems mainly. I sometimes use floppies for this, but that's pretty rare. One thing that has come up quite a lot is that the easiest way to get info into a virtual machine system is by applying a floppy drive image. This is because you need less than a megabyte of data. The system is programmed to turn on and then check the floppy drive for all its info on startup. These are of course not real floppy drives, but it means that all kinds of virtualisation systems still have a floppy driver, and they need it to boot up.

FT: **Virtualisation systems have never forgotten about floppy disks, but how about you? Have you always been interested in floppy disks? Or did you need to rekindle your interest in them at a point?**

FoT: It's a mix of both. There was a period when I didn't really care about them. As a kid, when floppies were still a thing, I got into computers and I was obsessed with them. Around the 2000s floppies kind of phased out and I stopped caring about them. I had computers that didn't have floppy drives and that didn't bother me. Around 2014 or so I got back into them, a lot harder this time.

FT: **How did this happen?**

FoT: I can actually narrow it down to a specific Tweet. I was getting back into some retro tech, because I had moved across the country and had gotten a new job. I was making a bit more money and I wanted to get the same Packard Bell I had as a kid. So, I started going onto eBay to look up a bunch of old retro stuff and bought some parts. It was then that the sci-fi author Charles Stross Tweeted about this one old computer he had – a Zenith minisPORT laptop, which had a unique floppy drive. It used a 2-inch floppy disk, which was only ever used by that one computer. They wanted to make the laptop smaller than any other, so they didn't have enough room to put in a full-size floppy drive. They shrunk the floppy drive and produced these really tiny, cute, odd little floppies instead. When I started looking into this it really got me interested in the medium.

FT: **Why is that do you think? What's the appeal of these odd floppies?**

FoT: I was around in the 90s and I thought I knew a lot about computers from that time, but I had never heard of this one. That took me down a rabbit hole of finding out the full breadth of floppy disk technology that I hadn't thought of before. Almost everyone at least recognises the floppy disk as a symbol, though maybe not as a physical thing. If you were around in the 90s, you know what a 3.5-inch floppy is. If you were around in the 80s, you know the 5.25-inch floppy and if you're even older you might have used 8-inch disks. The thing is that there were so many odd floppy formats made for different systems. There's a floppy disk that was only ever used on a Brother industrial sewing machine and one that only got used on some Japanese cash registers. So, unless you were in Japan or into sewing, you never saw these. It turns out, that floppy technology has gone down so many different paths that people don't know or remember. I think it's really interesting to show these.

FT: You decided to do this at festivals in the form of a self-curated floppy disk museum. How did this come about?

FoT: As I got more into collecting I figured that I should set up an exhibit for all the different types of floppy disks in my collection. I did this a couple of times at the Vintage Computer Festival at the Computer History Museum and at the Vintage Computer Festival up in Seattle. I don't really want to do the same display twice, so I constantly work on expanding the collection for the next year. I started with just a floppy disk exhibit, and then moved on to also doing an optical disk exhibit. I was kind of planning to move into flash media as well this year, but the festivals got cancelled due to the pandemic. I think that flash gets a lot more complicated and exciting as soon as you start looking at it more closely. The same can be said of optical media. When you think about them, you first consider CDs, DVDs, Blu-rays and maybe LaserDiscs, but there are actually all kinds of different, weird variations. There are shaped CDs and dual discs, which have data on both sides. There's the optical disc, which is a CD that's got vinyl on the other side. There is all kinds

of weird stuff that functioned as a stepping-stone on the way to other technologies.

FT: Why did you start with displaying the floppy disks in particular? What was the appeal?

FoT: A nice thing about a floppy collection is that it is very easy to pack up and take somewhere. I can just throw them all in a bin, put this in the car and go. What I really like about floppy disks, compared to other sorts of vintage tech, is that from the very beginning they were designed to be handled by humans. They expected people to be carrying them around and throwing them into their bags. A lot of times, when you look at vintage tech, you can't touch it, because it's too delicate. But with floppy disks you can just throw them around. You can have a table full of floppy disks and people can just pick them up and look at them. I think that is one of the things that made them so memorable. They're very tactile, but you're not going to break them just by holding them.

FT: The main output for your projects is a little less tactile. You mostly share your work online through Twitter. Why is that?

FoT: Well, I've looked into doing YouTube stuff as well and I do have a couple videos on my account. I also have a wiki, which I'm planning to expand. Still, I think Twitter is the medium that works best for me. It really comes down to the fact that I have ADHD and concentrating on something can be very hard. Something about the way Twitter works bypasses my ADHD block. The fact that Twitter limits you to three sentences helps me do things. I can't go back and edit endlessly and I also don't have to stare at a giant blank page. Some of the stuff I've written ended up on my blog, which is mainly just stuff from my Twitter, re-edited into longer posts. Twitter is perfect for the way I write; it fits with the way my brain works.

FT: You also get a lot of community input on Twitter. What kind of reactions do you receive?

FoT: The interesting thing is that people get the impression that I'm an electronics engineer. In reality, I just take a lot of pictures and Google some stuff. One of the things I do are these tech teardowns where I take apart some type of electronic device. Sometimes I'm 20 posts into the teardown and I've barely got the cover off, while other people might have already figured out what half the chips are. They reply to my posts and share their thoughts. I'm kind of crowdsourcing the wisdom of my followers as the threads go on. It's like I'm working in the middle of a room full of smart people who might be focusing on something else, but they can come over and go: 'Oh, yeah, you plugged that in backwards'.

FT: That sounds both nice and nerve-wracking. What are the downsides of these collective Twitter endeavours?

7.1 – Foone's Twitter handle as of 01.10.21.
Screenshot: Twitter

FoT: Well, sometimes I might do something and the thread ends up being 30 posts long. When I wrote something that was wrong and I correct myself later, people still correct me, because they stopped reading or never bothered deleting their Tweets. When I make a small mistake, I might get people correcting me for over a week. Recently I found an interesting ISA card inside a computer that I was taking apart. It turned out it was a canvas card from a German company. I thought it had the product name on it, but it was actually a postcode. I've had Germans correcting me on that one for the last week and I don't think they're stopping anytime soon.

FT: Is the online retro community a friendly one?

FoT: I think in a lot of ways, they're getting better. There were a lot of communities that were too small and too big at the same time. There's an unwritten law where if a community is small enough, there aren't any jerks there, because they can't afford to be. If the community has 15 million people the jerks get drowned out by the noise, because there are enough good people. I think, over the years, the retro tech community grew to the right size and has grown much bigger and healthier because of it.

FT: **Let's go into some of the hacks you've done. You call yourself a hardware/ software necromancer and have worked on several floppy related projects. For instance, you worked on a floppy disk image project using the Copy Pro 2000. What was that about?**

FoT: The Copy Pro 2000 was a device that was designed to duplicate floppies. The basic idea is that this is a standalone system. You put in a written floppy and then you just start feeding it blank floppies. It copies the first disk onto all the remaining ones. It's got some magic in there that makes it eject bad disks. So, you end up with a big pile of good floppies and hopefully, a smaller pile of bad ones. That's interesting, but not super useful nowadays, because the few projects that come out on floppy have relatively small runs. My idea was to take this thing apart, pull out the logic board and put in my own, so that it would image the whole disk before ejecting it. I ended up having to make a printed circuit board for that to work. So now, the disk comes out, stops, the machine takes a picture of the disk, and then it throws it out the rest of the way. In the end you have a bunch of virtual disk images, and a bunch of image files, so you can check what the disks look like and name them later. Once the project is done I'm able to throw in a hundred floppies and come back a couple hours later when they've all been imaged.

FT: **Another hack you did was the floppy keyboard. What's up with that?**

FoT: One of the things I like to do is to make keyboards that are obtuse and terrible to use. This started out by taking apart really cheap kids toys, like the ones from VTech. I would connect to their keyboard matrix and turn them into a real USB keyboard to use them on another computer. Later I started making keyboards on my own. I created one that's binary and only has two buttons; a zero and a one. You have to type out the digits. I also made one where you have just one button and you push it a number of times to type out the ASCII code of the key you want to type. I only made it through 'Hello', because my finger started hurting. I keep coming up with ideas for how to make a keyboard that's worse than the other ones. A while back I had a lot of floppy disks on hand, so I figured I'd make a floppy keyboard using a floppy drive connected to a Raspberry Pi. You put in a disk, which corresponds to a single key, it scans that disk and types that key for you. You can just type out whatever you want that way, really slowly. I'm currently working on a keyboard where I take the map of my local area and impose a keyboard overlay over it.

7.2 The inside of the Copypro 200 floppy disk duplication machine that Foone modified into a disk imaging tool.
Photo: Foone Turing

7.3 – Foone's demonstration of the floppy keyboard. Each floppy disk represents one keyboard character.
Photo: Foone Turing

The device is just a box with a button on it, and it's got a GPS inside. So, whenever I go somewhere, I can push it, and it takes the key based on the map. I have to drive all over the place to type maybe five letters. It's going to be a cross-America Tweet.

FT: What is the appeal of hacking retro technology like these keyboards?

FoT: I think that for a lot of people the interest comes from doing stuff that couldn't be done in the past, but can now be done as a limitation. Great creative work often happens not because of complete freedom, but due to limitations. Limitations mean

that you have to think outside of the box. Think of putting *Shrek* on a floppy disk as an example. There's no way you could have done that back in the day, but now that you've got really good compression algorithms these things become possible. Creativity comes out of a bottleneck. It turns out that floppy disks are a very well understood, common bottleneck. I think there's a David Byrne quote about how the characteristic of a medium is always the limitation of a medium. The quintessential electric guitar sound is distortion, because that's when you're playing too hard for the amplifier to handle the noise. The things you remember about a medium are its limitations. As technology progresses,

7.4 – Foone's floppy disk museum display at the Computer History Museum in Mountain View.
Photo: Foone Turing

you get fewer limitations, which is good in most cases, but also inherently less memorable. I think floppies are a particularly memorable sort of limitation, because everyone's going to understand that if you make something that fits onto a floppy you had to work really hard to make it happen.

FT: Where do your hacks end up after they are finished?

FoT: Well, a lot of them don't really end up anywhere other than on my Twitter. I've been meaning to put together some tutorials for my keyboard hacks, but often they end up being basically the same sort of

Arduino sketch with a couple of modified constants. Without also documenting how I wired them up, these can be difficult to rebuild. It's almost easier to recreate the thing from scratch. I got some stuff on my GitHub because it's open source, but usually I put it on Twitter and that's about it. It's one of the things I've been meaning to work on, but by the time I get stuff working most of my motivation is gone.

FT: Another thing you're known for is your collection of GIFs of floppy disks being used in anime. What do you find so interesting about this imagery?

FoT: I think that animation gives floppy disks an aesthetic that's very captivating. Almost universally, the animators don't draw an actual floppy, they draw something that looks like a floppy, but is different. It's someone's artistic interpretation of the thing. People put the notch on the wrong side, or they forgot how the actual shutter works, that kind of stuff. But the animated ones, they're not wrong; they're just not real. They decided to make them more interesting, by making them bigger or smaller, or they made them transparent. They did all kinds of stuff, just because they thought it looked cool, which I think gives an interesting edge to the medium.

FT: Do you think people nowadays look at floppies like that all the time, as something more interesting than what they actually were back in the day?

FoT: Floppies have kind of become a mythical thing from the past. You see that with people releasing music on floppies. That's not out of any kind of nostalgia for something that happened, because that was never a thing. I think these floppy disks reference more the mythic idea of the floppy than the actual physical object. One practical thing that is interesting about this is that it ties into the tendency for things to last far beyond their actual practical application, as symbols for something. Another example of this is the telephone symbol on your mobile phone. It's like some phone from the 70s; a big, clunky one with a huge handset. It has become the ideal representation of the phone, one that people recognise as a phone even when phones started getting different shapes and became cordless. Similarly, the save icon is a floppy disk. You don't need to know what a floppy disk is, you just need to know that this generic symbol is what we use as a save icon. Certain ideas make their way into culture and can just stay there forever. There will be people born decades after anyone has used a floppy disk, and they'll still think of it as a save icon.

FT: Do you see a future for the physical floppy disk, though?

FoT: The big limitation is the fact that no one makes them anymore. I've looked into ways to actually make new floppies, because at some point we're probably going to need them. There are a lot of old computers that need to use floppy drives and unless we replace them with emulators, we need actual floppies. The number of floppies in the world is constantly going down; it cannot go up at this point. We're moving away from physical media. Even things like hard drives are disappearing. Optical media, like Blu-ray, are also on their way out. I think we're moving increasingly towards an entirely flash and streaming world. I don't really see a lot of future for the floppy disk, outside of the nostalgia factor. But I think, conversely, this factor only goes up as they become less common. It's definitely getting to the point where they become a lot more indirectly nostalgic; a museum thing. They're kind of interesting in the same way as an old telegraph system. It's a neat science thing, even though you don't remember using it. As time goes on, that ratio of floppy disks is going to shift and the number of people still using them will decrease. Eventually, people will only remember them from museums and YouTubers talking about their history.

FT: What does that mean for you? Will you keep working with floppies, even if they become rare?

FoT: I think so. The stuff I do is only going to become more remarkable as it becomes more obscure. Fewer people might know about the things I talk about, but that also means I do something they might not have known yet. I think the research I do will only become more interesting with the passing of time.

'For me the diskmag is something that also connects us physically. The floppy disk has had a lot of influence on my social life.'

THE MAIN EVENT

SCENE WORLD is an eclectic NTSC & PAL diskmag that started out in 2001 and is still running today. It is kept active by an international group of enthusiasts, hailing from Peru, Germany, China, the USA, and the UK. New issues of the magazine are published regularly through their website, as executable files for Commodore 64 (C64) and Amiga.

We chatted with two members of Scene World to learn more about the legacy of the floppy disk in diskmags today. **JOERG DROEGE (JD)** *is the founder and main organiser of* Scene World, *while* **A J HELLER (AJ)** *works as an editor for* Scene World *and other diskmags, like* Vandalism News. *Let's find out how floppy disks can brisk up one's social life!*

Floppy Totaal (FT): Hello Joerg, hello AJ. Shall we start with a round of introductions? Can you tell us a little more about who you are?

AJ: Sure, my name is AJ Heller and I've been a demo coder, diskmag editor, and graphics guy on the C64 for what feels like a 1 000 years now. When I met Joerg about 20 years ago he dragged me into *Scene World*. We also do a podcast together. Besides that, I am an editor for *Vandalism News*, which is another diskmag that is still kicking around.

JD: I'm Joerg Droege and I'm the founder and main organiser of *Scene World*. I got a C64 when I was eight, back in 1990, because my grandfather used to have one. In 1998, I learned from *64'er magazine* about the demoscene and discovered that new games were still being released for the machine. When I found out that *Driven*, which was another diskmag, was dying, I figured it would be interesting to unite the two split NTSC and PAL user groups. I was always told it would be a waste of time, because there was nothing going on regarding C64 in Canada and the USA. I really had to convince people to go for the project.

FT: Is that where you came in AJ? How did the two of you meet?

AJ: Joerg contacted me when he was starting *Scene World*. Like he said, there was a prominent American diskmag called *Driven* that had kind of petered out. He wanted to continue it somehow by making a worldwide zine. Within the realm of diskmags and the demoscene, it's usually split between Europe and North America. In the old days, stuff that worked on European machines wouldn't necessarily work on American machines. Joerg wanted to put together a diskmag that encompassed everything and worked on all machines. He was looking around for somebody to edit the American part of it. I used to be an editor on *Driven* and I worked with a couple of European diskmags as well. Joerg emailed me and asked: 'Do you want to do this?' And I said: 'Maybe'.

JD: And he got stuck with it ever since!

FT: Let's rewind a little. Diskmags have been around for quite some time, but maybe not everyone is aware of their history. How would you describe a diskmag for someone who has never heard of the concept before?

AJ: Well, it's a magazine on a floppy disk. That's literally what it is. I've seen people just throw some text files on a disk and call it a magazine, but if you ask me that's just a bunch of text files on a disk. There needs to be some sort of presenter software; a magazine outfit as we call it at *Scene World*. Different diskmags have different names for it, but in essence it's always some way to present the text. Usually this is done through graphics and music, but sometimes also through software. That was *Loadstar's* big thing; there would be an article, and usually they would attach a piece of software to it. We don't do that so much with *Scene World*, though. We mostly do articles.

FT: What does the magazine outfit of Scene World look like?

JD: We go with just black and white graphics. We don't have fancy animations on the pages, because we try to be universal. You can control *Scene World* with the mouse, the joystick, and the keyboard. This is not typical for a diskmag. Usually it's joystick or keyboard only.

FT: What kind of content would you find in an issue of Scene World?

AJ: The magazines are usually pretty well stocked with text. We have several news chapters per issue. While we do try to keep everything together, we still split the news up into a separate European and American scene. We also have reviews for demos and games that have come out, and charts for who the best coders are. For this we send out a voting sheet before each issue. There are also tutorials. One of our coders is a prolific game designer and did some coding tutorials on how to make a game.

JD: We also have transcribed interviews. For example, the issue before the last one had an interview with John F. Kutcher who developed *Space Taxi*, which was one of the first games to have digital voice samples. Besides this, there are hardware reviews. That's the special thing about *Scene World* – we cover everything.

FT: That must be a lot of work. How do you prepare each issue?

AJ: It usually involves a lot of yelling and getting angry. We still develop everything on floppy disk when we put it all together. I don't know about other people, but I cannot work on non-original hardware. Some do a lot of coding through emulators. I can't get my brain around that. When I have an emulator on my laptop and I'm coding, I just open a web page to look at something and, before you know it, I'm watching YouTube videos and not actually doing any coding. If you're working on the C64, you're just doing what you're doing and that's it.

FT: The diskmag has a special relationship to the floppy disk. Can you describe it for us?

AJ: Well, there wouldn't be diskmags if there were no floppies, right? If it's not a diskmag, it's just a mag. My first encounter with diskmags was with *Loadstar*, which was an American magazine that was entirely on floppy disk. You could buy these on newspaper stands and in stores. I had a subscription to it and even ended up contributing over the course of a number of years. As a teenager I found it super awesome that I could just pop the magazine's floppy into my C64 and I would immediately see all the programs that were on it. Before that,

8.1 – The Scene World crew at their booth at Gamescom 2019. Photo: Joerg Droege

you would have an actual paper magazine and you had to type in all the programs. That was always a pain in the neck. Nobody liked doing that. Here it was already typed in for you. When I discovered the demoscene, not long after that, it just made sense to me that they also had diskmags.

FT: **Scene World is made for use on original hardware, but distributed as a disk image online. Is this very different from the past, when floppy disks were also shared through the post and magazines such as Loadstar?**

AJ: Back in the day I actually always went onto the Bulletin Board System (BBS) to download disk images and write them onto a disk. This was quite a similar process to what we currently have with *Scene World*. But of course, in the 80s and early 90s there was also an entire community built on swapping floppies. That's how you found a lot of old demos and other stuff that you didn't know about before. Aside from just swapping, there were swapping parties where a bunch of people would gather to make copies of their disks.

JD: In Germany BBS wasn't really a thing. Sending disks back and forth was more common than in America. I actually started as a swapper. It was pretty common to have a personalised note with every swapping package. When time got scarce people started writing mega-notes, which means you wrote one note to ten people.

Everyone would get a private message in the same note, and they could read the private message of everybody else. Imagine that nowadays. Those were different times. Nobody cared about privacy.

FT: **The floppy disk used to be pretty ubiquitous, up to the point that it still functions as an icon nowadays. Is the floppy disk a symbol that the entire diskmag community can get behind? Does it unite them as a group?**

AJ: The floppy disk does unite us as a diskmag, but I think that at this point we've known each other for so long that we've just become friends. Even if we stopped doing the magazine tomorrow, we'd still keep in touch.

JD: It was my reason for going to the USA and Peru. All the demoscene people from Lima I knew lived 15 minutes away from each other. In three weeks I hopped in a taxi from one friend to another. I had no problem communicating and I didn't get lost. I never thought I would have a friend in Peru, so for me the diskmag is something that also connects us physically. The floppy disk has had a lot of influence on my social life.

FT: **How many people work on Scene World at the moment?**

AJ: There are currently 20 people on staff. Sometimes it's like trying to herd cats to get everyone on board to do stuff and send things in on time. We've got certain people whose job it is to put everything together and sometimes they just disappear off the face of the earth. It has almost come to the point where we dread putting each issue together, because we know it's going to hurt.

JD: We are all in different time zones. AJ is six hours apart from me and we also have people in Peru and China. So, when I get up in the morning, they go to sleep. That's pretty difficult. It might take a day or two until we actually get an answer, but it can also take a week if there's a holiday or if China decides to block half the Internet again.

FT: How often does Scene World come out?

AJ: As soon as we release an issue, we try to organise the next one. It takes about a year for us to get it all together.

JD: There are also diskmags that only release one issue every five years. We mostly take our time, because we try to have exclusive music and we want things like an intro or logos and graphics in the text. What's special about floppy disk media compared to other media is that it's multimedia. That is why we have so many staff members. Bringing everything together is a lot of work. This process is called linking.

AJ: We've got some people that are just graphics guys, and some that are only musicians. They don't actually write any text for the magazine. There is also someone who has to edit the graphic layout of the directory, so that when you view the directory of the disk, it looks nice. There's a lot of stuff that goes into it. Especially now that we're doing the magazine for two different machines: C64 and the Amiga.

FT: How do you relate to other diskmags? Is this a friendly community?

JD: In the beginning, *Scene World* actually received a lot of negative feedback. People said that not solely covering the demoscene was a waste of time. Also, they said including the Americans and Canadians wasn't worth the bother and we shouldn't separate topics according to region. However, when we released our latest issue last year, people were celebrating. They'd turned around.

AJ: When we started, I was working on a couple of different diskmags, like *The Crest*, *Domination*, and *Vandalism*. When I mentioned *Scene World* some people were very dismissive of it. They felt it wasn't going to amount to anything. However, I sat out the first issue, because I wanted to see what these guys were going to come out with. After I saw the result, I felt like this was something that could go somewhere. So, I went in completely. At first *Scene World* was not met with open arms, but I think that through the 20 years of our existence the amount of people that are still making diskmags dwindled. Because of this the animosity that may have existed before doesn't exist anymore. At this point, if anybody is continuing the tradition, people tend to love it.

8.2 - A selection of opening menus collected from *Scene World* and *Loadstar*. Source: Scene World

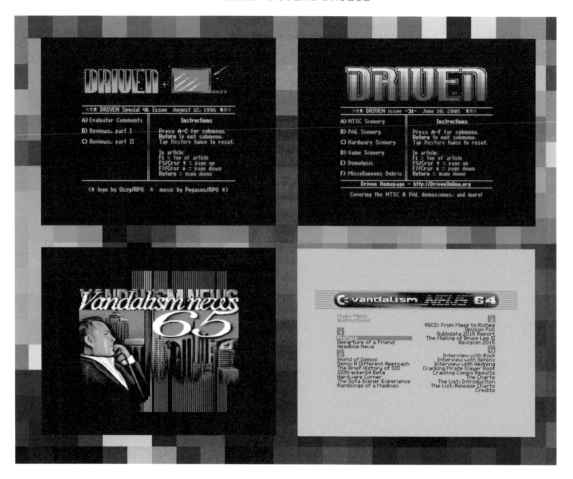

8.3 - Some opening menus from *Driven* and *Vandalism.* Source: Scene World

FT: **Can you tell us a little more about the fact that your magazine is both NTSC and PAL? What was your motivation for combining the two?**

JD: The main problem 20 years ago was that there was no standard for a diskmag that could run on all machines. Nobody was trying to develop a floppy loader that automatically detects if you have an American or a European machine. What for? It would simply crash. I wanted our diskmag to run despite the machine you're using, not just by luck. I think that we are responsible for the fact that in the last ten years most games released for the C64 are NTSC fixed. I don't recall any commercially released game from that time on, which would crash on NTSC. Well, aside from *Farming Simulator*...

AJ: The point is that *Scene World* made the American scene visible again. At the time a lot of games were being released that didn't run on American machines, and if they did, it wasn't a real fixing job. The music would still be way too fast and the gameplay would be way off. All they cared about was that the game didn't crash. Now they see that there is a market in the US for people that still want to play these games. So, they'll go through that extra effort to make sure that it runs well.

JD: Which means we are now in better times than we were in the 80s or 90s!

FT: **What else is different for diskmags now compared to 20 years ago?**

AJ: Accessibility is number one. 30 years ago, you had to get your diskmag off of BBS, which would take three hours to download, and then you had to convert the file to a disk to read it. The audience for the diskmag was limited to the people that had the hardware to do this. Now, if you don't have the hardware, you can just read it with an emulator, right on the website. The amount of people that experience the diskmag is much higher now than it was back in the 90s. Communication was also limited. Now, we can just do a Skype chat and get the people in the magazine together to sit down and discuss things. Getting stuff around has become way easier. There's so much more you can do, even with the old hardware, that you couldn't do before. My C64 is attached to my Wi-Fi network now, for instance.

FT: **What is the appeal of using the C64 today? It sounds like it has become a pretty hybrid affair. Why would you keep repurposing this old hardware?**

JD: Well, I totally adore the SID music. One of the best things about our diskmag is the exclusive tunes we have every time. I also like games that push the limits of the hardware. For example, some time ago *Sam's Journey* was released. We had an exclusive English interview with Chester Kollschen who coded that. There's still new hardware and software being produced for the C64. That's my reason to stick with it.

AJ: I've been in the C64 scene since the early 90s and I think the machine is still a tool that can be used for creating something. When people say it's obsolete, I say paint is also pretty obsolete, but people still paint. I was always a graphics guy and a coder. The medium that I would create with was the C64. It's an older machine, but it's still capable of quite a bit and I don't think that it's anywhere near the end of its lifespan. There's still plenty that we can do with it.

FT: One argument that pops up a lot in favour of using floppy disks is that the medium can function as a sort of creative limitation. Is this the same for you?

AJ: Yeah, you've got a limited palette. The C64 is still the main medium through which I create graphics and stuff. When I swap over to a Mac and go to a graphics program, I simply don't know where to start with it. When you have a 4k display, how do you pixel in a logo? There's no way. Whereas on a C64 I've got 320 x 200 pixels and 16 colours. Creating graphics with these limitations, pixel by pixel, is doable. A lot of times, when you're using certain logo editors, you're even limited to three colours. What draws me to this is trying to make something where you don't see those limitations, where you would never guess that it's only three colours.

FT: Let's talk a bit about Scene World's audience. It sounds like there are a lot of different groups involved. Who reads the magazine in the end?

JD: We did an estimate once and we had about 3 000 downloads of a *Scene World* disk image on the Commodore scene data-base. Since we now have our diskmag on the homepage we don't have all the numbers anymore. There were many requests from people who wanted to check the magazine at work, which is why we also emulate it.

AJ: We've been working to expand the number of people that can read *Scene World*. We've released an Amiga version, which is essentially the same, but on a different platform. Aside from that, we have an emulated version of the magazine that you can read right on the web page. Before, you would need to have either an emulator or actual hardware to do that. Now, anybody who has a web browser can view it there. We've also been trying to expand *Scene World* with things like a podcast. We do historical interviews, some Twitch streaming and stuff like that. All of this is to push people towards the diskmag itself. I think that the amount of people that are willing to download and listen to a podcast is probably higher than those that are willing to figure out how to make a diskmag work.

FT: Wouldn't it make sense to focus even more on the accessible content?

JD: Last year, when we participated at the Gamescom festival, we had 500 more subscribers on the podcast that week. Still, we wouldn't even have had a booth at the event if we didn't have the

8.4 - AJ and Joerg working together on *Scene World*. Photo: A.J Heller

diskmag and kept working with floppy disks. It's what sticks in people's heads.

AJ: The diskmag is the main event, the other stuff just expands on it. I think that there are a lot more viewers and listeners of the historical stuff and the podcast than there are people that actually read the magazine, but the purpose of these is to nudge them towards the magazine.

FT: Couldn't you present something similar to the diskmag through other media though? What is the modern-day equivalent of the floppy disk?

AJ: Of course, there are ways to translate it. Recently, SD cards have been a big thing in the demoscene. You can put a disk image on there and pretend to have a floppy disk, but there's nothing quite like an actual floppy disk. I think SD cards serve a good purpose, but I don't use them for emulating a disk. I use them for archiving disks, when I make a backup. It's the same as back in the late 80s and early 90s when there were hard drives available for the C64. Essentially, I use the SD card as a hard drive. Before I use the disk images, they're written back to a floppy disk. There's something that feels more tactile when using a floppy disk. When these games or software were made, that's what they had in mind. So, to remove that, to take that out of the equation, kind of ruins the experience.

FT: What does the future of the diskmag look like?

AJ: I don't think it's going away anytime soon; we're still committed to producing it in the future. As long as there is a scene that is receptive to diskmags, they will continue to be produced. *Scene World* has 19 people involved, so if one person hangs it up, that's okay. We go on. It would take a mass exodus of people for us to quit, and that's unlikely to happen. For now, we would like to start doing more Amiga centric stuff and we'll keep expanding the software that we're using. We've been talking about rebuilding the presenter for the magazine for a while. That's my number 23 priority right now.

FT: Where do you think the floppy disk will be in ten years time?

JD: It will be very hard to find. Even now you see people on eBay paying €40 or €50 for used disks in a shabby state. 20 years ago, getting a floppy disk wasn't a problem. The problem was getting people to work on solutions to make things useable on all systems. Nowadays, people have the solutions, but getting the disks is becoming problematic. The biggest problem is mould. Many people put their floppies in their attic or cellar. It takes half an hour just to clean the mould off one disk. I only do that for very rare, original disks that I want to preserve. I always check if a disk was stored correctly over the years before I buy it.

AJ: They will start to degrade over time. I've got some brand new floppies that are 30

years old, but even those might not work in
future. The hardware required to use floppy
disks is dwindling as well. A lot of these
things are belt driven. Commodore drives
use specific mechanisms and you can't just
grab another mechanism from somewhere
and stick it in there. At some point, you're
simply going to run out of things to use
the floppy disks on, even if they still work.
There's a finite lifespan to what we're doing.

FT: **That raises one final question:
what happens to the diskmag if
there are no more floppies?**

AJ: Well, we'd have to become
a disk image magazine.

JD: We'd use the same constraints.
The emulation would still need to
look like a real disk image.

AJ: Unless we'd somehow just use an entire
SD card, but that would be too lame.

'One of my friends said that the floppy is the holy grail of independent music, as if the entire underground was waiting for the medium to appear.'

AN UNDERGROUND ADVENTURE

ADAM FRANKIEWICZ (PL) makes sure he isn't defined by just one genre or activity; amongst many things he is a theatre director and a contemporary electronic composer. These activities led to the founding of his independent record label Pionierska Records in 2014, which has been publishing music exclusively on floppy disk since 2018. At the time of writing, the Pionierska Records library consists of over 35 releases by almost as many artists. Adam also spreads his enthusiasm for floppy disk culture through his online floppy disk news channel Floppy (Not) News and by conducting floppy based workshops throughout Europe.

We wanted to find out more about Adam's experiences running a floppy disk label and Pionierska's position in the current music landscape. This is what he had to say.

Floppy Totaal (FT): Hi Adam, how are you doing? Working on any new floppy projects?

Adam Frankiewicz (AF): Hey there! It's been a busy time. I'm still releasing things and finding out about new stuff. In the last two or three days I found a really nice website with utilities for DOS. I bought a small computer to practice on: a Toshiba Libretto. It has a Yamaha OPL3 SA3 Sound Chip inside. So now I can make music on a real DOS machine, back from the time when floppies were the main thing.

FT: Will you release this new music on floppy through Pionierska?

AF: Yes, I'm currently preparing for this, though I should mention I've released only two floppies of my own music so far. With the label I mostly focus on releasing music from other artists. Running the label is a huge honour for me. People trust me to do a good job.

FT: Can you tell us a little more about how the label is run? How many floppies do you put out per release?

AF: We are not a real business in any way; we only make 20 floppies each time. Five go to the artists, one goes into my catalogue and 14 are sold to cover expenses. This includes the floppies themselves and the printing. We don't put a lot of money into promotion. The floppy scene is a small world.

FT: Were you always into floppies? What was your first computer?

AF: When I was about nine years old I got an Amiga. My friends already had PCs back then, but my parents didn't have the money to buy me one. I was always trying to find out where to buy floppies. There was this second-hand shop in the centre of my hometown, Łomża, where they sold a lot of different second-hand tech. The guy who ran it brought boxes full of floppies from Germany and Holland. The text on the labels was in German, so we didn't know what was on them. I would try to collect full games, which was like three floppies for one game, by looking for labels with the same name.

FT: Were you also interested in music back then?

AF: Yes, when I was 14 years old I fell in love with a girl who was in a punk group, and so I also needed to start a band and become a punk. The band was called W Spadku Po Dziadku, which means 'Inheritance From My Grandfather'. We had Lenin on the front cover – so punk! I think it was at the academy where I studied puppetry in the Theatre Department, around 2005, that I learnt how to use programs like Ableton Live and started exploring electronic music. I liked the possibilities of the software. It felt like a very open world.

FT: Was it difficult to meet similar minded people back then?

AF: There was not a lot of communication between different kinds of experimental groups in Poland at the time. I was really obsessed with knowing everything that was going on and telling people about it. I travelled around and everywhere I went I would ask: 'Where's the underground? Where are people playing?' This was the easiest way to find nice places and people. I didn't stop and moved from subculture to subculture. A friend of mine said to me that he'd never seen a person change subcultures as many times as I have.

FT: Couldn't you also connect to these subcultures through the Internet?

AF: For me, the Internet was just a place where you downloaded something. I didn't actually spend time on it like I do now. Currently I live on the Polish seaside in a very small city called Kołobrzeg and I don't travel very much. Sharing information and talking about floppies online enables me to travel through different means. I think a medium like the floppy can be a door to different communities. In that way it is quite similar to the cassette.

FT: Pionierska was first a cassette label, right? How did you get into cassettes?

AF: A friend of mine suggested releasing the music for a theatre piece we did together. Putting it out on cassette was his idea, because he had a very old car with a cassette deck inside it and he wanted to listen to the music in there. I remembered cassettes from my punk times. They were pretty cool and cheaper than CDs. Back then I was living at Pionierska street, so this became the label name. I didn't think about the fact that Pionierska also means pioneer.

FT: Do you feel like a pioneer? Were there other cassette labels around in Poland at the time?

AF: Yes, but I didn't know them very well. After we established the label, they started writing to ask if we wanted to swap tapes with them. Selling tapes can be very difficult, so people swap them. There's an entire culture around this. The label picked up pretty fast. We started selling cassettes at cassette flea markets. We sold them for around €2, 50 or €3 each. Everybody else had prices like €6 or €7. I didn't know cassettes could be so expensive!

FT: How did Pionierska become a floppy label?

AF: After the first 18 tape releases my friends dropped out of the label and I was the only one left. I decided to keep on going with the project. People sent me demos and I really liked them. I thought it was a good opportunity to release new music. I started thinking about a new medium for the label, because my cassette decks were completely broken by then. I remembered that on one of the German floppies from the second-hand shop there was a song that was like four or five minutes long and it sounded very good. So, I checked the Internet to figure out how this was possible and read about mod files. I thought, okay, so this is a good medium!

FT: Can you give us some examples of the artists that have released something on your label?

AF: At the very beginning I wanted to bring together as many generations of musicians on the label as possible. I started the series with famous Polish experimental musicians, such as Łukasz Szałankiewicz, who is a member of the Polish Society for Electroacoustic Music and the Polish Society for Contemporary Music. Another artist we released is Tomasz Mirt, a multi-instrumentalist, graphic artist, and painter. He used to lead the record label cat sun, and is now publishing field recordings as part of Saamleng. I also tried to release debuts, like those of DJ Lotos, my dear friend and one of my favorite Warsaw Trance musicians. He is also involved in theatre music and is an audio engineer. A final example is Aborygen, another extraordinary character that creates wonderful compositions using general-midi. There are so many great artists who work on the borders between art and music.

FT: It must be quite a challenge making their music fit on a disk?

AF: The most important thing is that the artists figure out how to work with the limited storage capacity of 1.4 MB. It's going

back in time; people really need to connect to the medium. One way to make the music fit is by working with trackers instead of compressed sound. All tracker programs originate from the need to create and code music for computer games. The first tracker ever made is probably The Ultimate Soundtracker, created by Karsten Obarski, for Amiga computers. Of course, over time, new versions were created that adopted the same way of writing notes and commands. Some examples of tracker formats are MOD (Sound / Noise / Fast / ProTracker), XM (Fast Tracker II), IT (Impulse Tracker), S3M (Scream Tracker 3), but there are many, many others.

FT: You also compress audio so it can fit on the disks. What tools do you use to do this? And what other formats besides mp3 do you prefer?

AF: All lossy formats have their advantages and disadvantages; the ogg format and a dedicated program oggdropXPd are the best for my needs. ogg works perfectly with low bitrates. Unlike mp3, it deals with so-called per-ear compression. The bitrate is lower, but the algorithm is great at intelligently negotiating between what the human hears and what the machine formats.

FT: Where do you find the actual floppies? Do you buy most of them online?

AF: Yes, on eBay, but also on the second-hand market. People sell these huge boxes at very, very low prices, like

9.1 - Adam conducting one of his floppy workshops during Floppy Totaal in 2019. Photo: Thomas Walskaar

a 1 000 disks for 600 zł, which is about €125. You can still buy large quantities of floppy disks very cheaply online.

FT: Did you get into contact with other floppy labels when you started Pionierska?

AF: The first floppy label I found on the Internet was Strudelsoft from the USA. They mostly release floppies with compressed music using the mp3 format. Other labels I like and respect are Wrieuw Recordings, Gulf Audio Company, Floppy Kick, Diskette Etikette Rekords, MAV records, Loser Crew Recordings and tmrw>. Before I started Pionierska I had a very nice conversation with the guy from Floppy Noise Records in the Ukraine. I asked him how the floppy sales were going and he said 'slowly'.

FT: Did this demotivate you?

AF: No, he might not have realised it, but this actually encouraged me! After my first release I started selling floppies very, very fast. The feedback on the Internet was huge. I was quite surprised. A month later one of my friends said that the floppy is the holy grail of independent music, as if the entire underground was waiting for the medium to appear.

FT: Why do you think Pionierska's floppy disks were such a success? What is the appeal of the medium?

AF: I think there was a demand for an independent medium that isn't connected to any business in the underground scene. People were looking for new ideas. They didn't want to release vinyl records, because it was too expensive. I think that everybody was looking for a medium that could be something very unique and through which they could express themselves. Small is beautiful, that's why the floppy might have become the next thing.

FT: Can you tell us a little bit more about what inspires the design of the Pionierska releases? You prepare all the artwork yourself, right?

AF: Yes, I did. I started by researching how floppies were released in the past, especially in the 80s and 90s, but also by other labels that operate now. I like the shape of the floppy. It's very hard to get right; not a perfect square and with a lot of angles. I made sketches to figure out how to deal with all these lines. For the first ten releases I just focussed on black and white covers. This simplicity worked with the shape of the floppy somehow. I want people to be interested in them. The design can push people to buy the disks and engage with them.

FT: Could the floppy disk become too successful, like vinyl or cassettes?

AF: Well, cassettes used to be a medium for independent groups, but now I see them being eaten up by music companies.

9.2 - From Adam's home studio, where every release is hand-copied and assembled. Photo: Adam Frankiewicz

The same happens with every culture that comes from the underground. Companies are always looking for things that are currently growing and then they take them over. That's why there should be a medium that will never catch on.

FT: So you think the floppy disk is not marketable?

AF: No, because people like it in a different way. It's more like a phenomenon. The floppy is dedicated to a very precise culture and can't be pushed beyond its limits. These limitations will keep people from making money out of it. Not everybody wants to work with 1.44 MB. I feel that the people that work with the medium have a very special love for it, a certain sensitivity for something that is passing.

FT: Where do you think this sensitivity comes from?

AF: I think it's a combination of the times in general and the fact that those who like floppy disks are hitting a certain age. They start to have more stability in life and look at their roots, to investigate what created them. However, they are not looking at their families, but at their floppies. I think that for every object that you can hold in your hand there is a huge culture of people who like to focus on it and generate ideas from it. If the object can handle some information, like the floppy, the scene will be even bigger.

FT: I wonder, how does Pionierska relate to the historical floppy subcultures, such as the demoscene?

AF: Back in the 90s there were these small groups of people that released their music on disks. They would create really nice floppies with software through which you could listen to mod files. They would copy them and send them out for free. This was a really important thing. Swappers would copy floppies and send them to other groups of people through the pre-Internet network. For them this was very natural. However, they are no longer doing this in the same way. I'm now on some demo-scene groups on Discord. When I show them what we do with Pionierska, they like it, but they always ask: 'Why not do it on a normal medium? Why don't you release music on CDs?' The mod culture is now totally different. They have FTP servers where all original modules can be downloaded for free. When you go back to the disk like I do, I think they feel resentful that a young guy wants to do what they did 20 years ago. Maybe they feel that it's part of retro culture. Some of them don't like that.

FT: Why do you think that is?

AF: They see retro culture as a totally different thing from what they do. It generates money by creating brand new objects to sell to people who like things from the past. The prices are really high. When I started working with floppies, I just stuck to my price of €3, 50. That's just enough to

9.3 - The Pionerska Records catalogue. All floppies are carefully categorised and stored in this folder.
Photo: Adam Frankiewicz

cover expenses and nothing more. I know that the people from the Hungarian Floppy Kick label sell their floppies for €1 or just 50 cents. That's crazy and I love it. I hope we can keep this vibe in the floppy scene. People love to have a floppy disk, but there should be a limit to how much you ask for one. It's a very old medium, prepared for new usage, so you shouldn't ask €25 for it.

FT: On the one hand you say that people like floppies out of nostalgia, but on the other hand you want to oppose retro culture. Isn't this a contradiction?

AF: I see retro culture as just reselling the goods from the past. This is different from what Pionierska tries to do. Retro culture doesn't re-assemble or push the medium somewhere new. Just look at the Gameboy scene. You can still buy an old Gameboy for €25 on the Internet if you search for it, but there are also companies who make a profit by producing new stuff based on the toy. I'd say, give the Gameboy a second life, but in the simplest way possible. Don't use people's nostalgia to make money.

FT: Pionierska's releases have a very limited 'print run'. I understand that you don't want to make money from your floppies, but a side-effect of this limited run is the limited accessibility of your releases. How do you feel about this scarcity?

AF: Well, before anything the label should be fun and interesting. My primary goal

is to sell floppies, without turning it into a business. I am not interested in selling digital files, which is why I ask €666, 00 for a download on Bandcamp. When the floppies sell out, people can still stream the tracks, but they cannot buy the music. I like Bandcamp because you can listen to music without anybody earning money from it. It's not the same as the micro donations on Spotify, which I really dislike.

FT: Does listening to music on Spotify create a different experience than listening to a floppy released by Pionierska?

AF: When I listen to music, I always give attention to the medium the music comes on. There were many years in which I just collected tapes from different places. When you want to try out a tape, you have to buy a tape deck. It's an extra step you have to take. I really like it when people make this kind of effort, because this takes them on a journey. I think it's strange if you don't make this investment, but something is just pushed on you, like on Spotify. It's not a platform that I choose to listen to. I think choosing to stream is like choosing nothing. The algorithm does the job for you. You need somebody to send you some- thing different, to change the algorithm. Without this, you're just living in a bubble.

FT: In a way, simply by running Pionierska, you fight the floppy's obsolescence. Do you think that the floppy disk could ever truly die? Or will people keep using them?

AF: I've never seen a new player being produced for a piece of old technology, like VHS or cassette. Certain media will get lost if we don't repair our old stuff. Many people just throw out old media players or don't want to put any effort into repairing something that is broken. It's good to think about what you have lying around. It doesn't have to take up too much space on the shelf. If it's broken, you can repair it.

FT: What are your future goals with Pionierska? Anything you still hope to achieve?

AF: I'm happy if we can cover costs and keep on releasing floppies. Nowadays, I ask people to work on their own artwork, because I think that if more people are involved, more floppies will go to people who participate in releasing them and not just buyers or collectors. It's like we're doing it for ourselves. I'm comfortable with just doing the things that I like and generating fun out of it.

FT: What do you see as the future of floppy music labels? Will they last?

AF: Well, a week ago I was talking to my friend Kamiel, who started releasing floppies on his label *tmrw>* . He's buying these very nice plastic covers from China, where they still produce them. They have a very cool design. He told me that Pionierska is what influenced him to start his label, so the floppy virus is spreading.

FT: How about you and your future?

AF: Floppies are my adventure. I will keep releasing them as long as I have the time for it and people still support Pionierska. But if not, I will find a new medium that can generate interest for me. I don't depend on it to earn a living; I do it because I like it. I want to stay an independent label and not grow. Through the medium you will always find new, interesting people and you will always know that they're cool. They'll always be your friends, because there is no money involved. For now, I still have thousands of floppies lying around waiting for new projects and artists!

'I think my interest baffles friends and family, so it was nice to discover an online community that finds what I do interesting.'

LOST AND FOUND

JASON CURTIS (UK) is a no-nonsense writer, librarian, and collector from Shropshire, England. In 2006 he founded the Museum of Obsolete Media, a formidable collection of media formats consisting of over 700 audio, video, data, and film objects. The collection includes many examples of unconventional and obsolete formats, which are carefully investigated and then documented on the museum's website. Among these, several unusual versions of the floppy disk can be found, providing insight into the alternative history of the medium.

We asked Jason about these obscure formats and the workings behind obtaining and maintaining an obsolete media collection. What can this teach us about the way we handle our media today?

Floppy Totaal (FT): Hi Jason, we're very glad to have this interview with you! How are you doing today?

Jason Curtis (JC): I'm doing fine, thank you. What shall we talk about first?

FT: I think the best place to start is the Museum of Obsolete Media. How did the museum come about? When did you start collecting?

JC: Well, I started my collection in 2006, while living in the south of England. My idea was to collect some examples of media that I had used over the years and that were starting to disappear. In my lifetime I've used things like 8-tracks, cassette tapes, and Philips VCR cassettes. At first, I imagined that I would have a collection of maybe 30 to 50 different formats, but then I also started gathering a few examples of formats I hadn't used myself. By 2013, I had collected several hundred different formats and I wasn't really sure what to do with them all. I decided to start the website, and carried on from there.

FT: The museum has grown quite a bit since then.

JC: Yes, I suppose it has its own momentum now. It expanded way beyond what I ever imagined. The collection just kept on growing. Because it has become quite well known I've received a lot of donations. I thought that when I got near 400 different formats, I wouldn't get much further than that. Now I'm almost at 750 and there seems to be no end to it, really.

FT: Why is it important to collect and share information on older media, especially now?

JC: I think partly it's about making people aware of the variety of media available, some of which is very obscure. It is also about helping people identify media that they may own, either personally, or perhaps in an archive. My ratings for media stability and player obsolescence may help guide decisions on the urgency of transcribing or migrating media formats, though I recognise that this is a huge area that the Museum only really touches on. Hopefully, by collecting the media, writing about them, and signposting to further information sources or to companies that can transcribe media formats, I'm doing a little bit to aid the preservation of information held on obsolete media.

FT: Can you tell us what the Museum of Obsolete Media currently looks like offline?

JC: In a physical sense it consists of stacks of plastic boxes containing various types of obsolete media, which I'm trying to gradually sort. A particular box will have, say, consumer videotape, or broadcast videotape, or memory cards. The materials fill up quite a lot of boxes and spaces in the house now. At some point I'd like to move to a slightly bigger house with a separate room for the collection. For now, it is still manageable, though. One of the perks of collecting just the media and not the devices that play them is that it saves a lot of space. I don't have to pay for storage or anything like that. I can fit several dozen formats in a small box.

FT: Were you ever tempted to also collect the devices that played the obsolete media?

JC: There are some formats for which I bought the device as well, but only because I had to purchase them together. I now own a number of dictation devices, for instance. But in the main, I try to buy just the media to save space and money on postage. That way the collection doesn't become too unwieldy.

FT: Is there a system behind how you categorise your collection online?

JC: It has developed over time really. In the beginning I split the collection up into audio, video, and data. I started collecting film formats later. I subdivided data into things like disks, tapes, ROM cartridges, and so on. It's my own classification system that I've adapted over the years. One of the things I'm trying to work on at the moment is to divide the collection even further through different types and sizes. So, for floppy disks, you've got the 5.25-inch, 3.5-inch, less than 3.5-inch, etc.

FT: Is it important that your collection is neatly categorised? Do you see yourself as an archivist while doing this?

JC: Yes, I suppose it satisfies my desire for order. It's quite nice to have things categorised and listed in different ways so that people can find them. I use tags quite a lot on the site as well and I've got plugins that will enable you to find similar formats. We have no control over the way things are, but at least we have some control over the way things are ordered. At my job as a librarian, people come along, and they can mess up the shelves and stuff. But in my collection, I can have it exactly as I like, which is quite satisfying.

FT: What media do you find the most interesting to collect? Are all formats equally exciting?

JC: I suppose the formats I have the strongest connection to are the ones that I have used myself in the past. So, things like the Phillips VCR videocassettes, or the 5.25-inch floppy disk. I also like strange things like the RCA Selectavision that played CED videodisks. They were around in the 80s, but I don't remember hearing about them back then. Basically, they are vinyl disks that look like a record in a caddy and they hold mainstream movies and music videos. I find them really intriguing. You've also got real oddities like the Tefifon, which is just such a bizarre idea. It's got grooved belts that play like a record, but is an endless plastic tape in a cartridge. There are some really weird and wacky things in the museum.

FT: When we think about floppy disks, most people think of the 3.5-inch

10.1 – Jason Curtis at his desk, where most of the work for the museum is done. Photo: Jason Curtis

floppy, which became the standard for a long time. Can you give us some examples of alternative floppy disks that people might not be aware of?

JC: There are actually a number of different sorts of floppy disks that I didn't know about until recently. For instance, there is the 3.25-inch disk or 'Flex Diskette', which looks like a shrunken 5.25-inch disk. I found out about this one a couple of years ago when somebody donated one to the collection. There's also a disk for a Sharp palmtop computer called the Pocket Disk that doesn't seem to be used in any other device. Then there's a rare Hungarian floppy disk, which is called the 'MCD cassette', and has quite a thick case. It looks a bit like a 3-inch floppy disk and it was invented in the 70s, but never got marketed until the early 80s. It was far ahead of its time, but was never really commercially developed.

FT: What is the appeal of these 'failed' formats?

JC: They're sort of interesting in the way they fit into the whole history of media. Why did these come about? I think my interest baffles friends and family, so it was nice to discover an online community that finds what I do interesting. It's just intriguing that they exist. There are computers that might have been on sale for less than a year. The Mattel Aquarius for example, was sold for about four months. It's also a challenge to find these things and research them, trying to uncover their background.

FT: Do you think there is an overarching reasoning behind the development of these alternative formats?

JC: Maybe somebody just tried to be different for difference sake. It could also be that they felt that their format met a need. When you think about the Tefifon, the idea behind its invention might have been that it played for a very long time and the sound quality is reasonably good. I suppose the company also didn't have to pay licencing fees to anybody. It was its own invention. There must have been some reasoning behind it, though it's hard to know exactly what it was.

FT: Where does your personal fascination for these relatively unknown media come from?

JC: It's hard to say. I find the design of these objects interesting. I remember as a child, looking at compact cassettes and wondering why they were made the way they are.

What were the different notches for? What were they about and how did they work? When I was young, my granddad bought an old Phillips VCR videocassette recorder. At the time nobody had them – everyone had either VHS or Betamax. So, we had this really unusual video recorder that played these strange tapes with lots of flaps and doors in them. I think that's partly where my interest in alternate media started.

FT: Were you already working with media before you started the Museum?

JC: I've worked as a librarian for the last 25 years. In the course of that time, I've come across a lot of different media that today are quite unusual, like ZIP disks, QIC mini-cartridge tapes, and networked CD-ROMs. At the time, we just used them without really thinking about it. Suddenly you realise that these objects are disappearing and it'd be nice to keep hold of some of them.

FT: Was this also the case with the floppy disk? Did you see those disappear?

JC: I remember when I worked in a medical library in London, we'd have so many floppy disks in the lost property box. They were ubiquitous, really – everybody had a floppy disk to save his or her work on; there was no cloud storage or anything like that. Suddenly, around 2002, they began to disappear, until we had no floppy disks in lost property anymore. Everybody had moved to USB drives.

FT: Even though floppy disks are deemed obsolete they can still be found nowadays There are even artists and programmers that specifically work with them. Why do you think that is?

JC: Perhaps it's the challenge – seeing what you can get onto such a small format, given that nowadays, you can fit gigabytes onto an SD card. It's interesting to see if you can do something creative with a fraction of the storage space. Maybe it's also an historical thing. The floppy disk has always been there, in the background. As a save icon, it's still around. They hail from a time that people remember, perhaps even from using them in their youth. When I went to university, floppy disks were quite a big deal, and quite expensive. I remember buying my first 5.25-inch floppy disk back in 1990. About a year or so later, I bought an Amstrad word processing machine that used 3-inch floppy disks. Even at the time that seemed quite unusual, they weren't the popular size.

FT: Where do you find information about an obscure format such as the 3-inch disk?

JC: Initially, I relied quite a lot on Wikipedia, but there are many formats that aren't on there at all. So, I really have to do the background research. Being a librarian helps. I find things on Google Books, like magazine articles. Sometimes I also get references from people, on Twitter for instance.

FT: Do you feel that you are part of a larger online community with an interest in media archaeology?

JC: Yes, I would say so. Starting the Twitter feed particularly helped me to get in contact with people who have an interest in a similar area and I had no idea there were so many. I've been in touch with people from all around the world. I sent a package to somebody in India today and I've also posted stuff to America and Russia. I think my interest baffles friends and family, so it was nice to discover an online community that finds this interesting.

FT: Did you discover any obsolescent media you didn't know about through these online interactions?

JC: On occasions I've had people contact me to say they've got some unusual piece of media laying around. They don't know what it is and they ask if I can identify it. Sometimes I have been able to do so and other times I've had to go to Twitter and ask. It seems to provoke quite a lot of interest when someone's got something really unusual, and no one seems to know what it is. People have managed to identify things on Twitter that I didn't know about myself. That's quite helpful.

FT: It seems like this online community is quite friendly. Do you also help each other out with the actual collecting process?

10.2 – A screengrab of The Museum of Obsolete Media's homepage. Source: obsoletemedia.org

JC: That has happened. For example, I've agreed with somebody not to bid on something and vice versa. Also, people have kindly pointed out eBay auctions that I didn't know about. I've done a few cooperative purchases with people. Recently, a friend of mine bought a dictation machine with a set of tapes. I chipped in, together with someone else, and he sent the tapes out to us. It doesn't happen very often, but I think we'll probably have more of that in the future.

FT: **It seems the Internet is very important for finding information about obsolescent media and connecting to other people. Is there also some offline activity, like special collector events or flea markets?**

JC: If there are events like that, I'm not aware of them. Most of my collection comes from eBay and I often buy things from overseas. Occasionally I find things at antique markets, but not very often. Most have the same type of material you see all the time. I think without eBay, I wouldn't have a much of a collection. It'd be very, very hard to do this.

FT: **Are there any formats you are still looking for?**

JC: I have an extensive wanted list! I thought originally that it would get shorter over time, but it's the opposite – it gets longer and longer. That's partly because people keep suggesting things I haven't got and partly

10.3 – A Sharp Pocket Disk from 1986.
Source: Museum of Obsolete Media

10.4 – A 3.25-inch floppy disk by Dyson
Source: Museum of Obsolete Media

because of me finding stuff that I've never heard of. People sometimes donate objects and I still search through eBay from time to time to see if I can find anything from my wanted list. I have lots of 'Saved Searches' set up. Occasionally these objects do crop up, but often it will take years and years to find something. Sometimes I think I'll never find an item and then suddenly I do.

FT: Are there any floppies left on your wish list?

JC: Yes, I think there are. One area that interests me is the whole idea of super floppies and floppy replacement disks, such as Sony's HiFD. People were trying to invent a replacement for the floppy disk. When they made the new version of the floppy, they replicated the shape and function of it, and

even the name, for instance, with the video floppy. There was a whole culture around mimicking the floppy disk. In the end these were all swept away by CDs and USB sticks.

FT: In a way, this mimicking of the floppy disk is still going on. There is a lot of contemporary merchandise that references the floppy disk. You can buy USB sticks in the shape of floppy disks, for example, or floppy shaped coasters. How do you feel about this?

JC: I don't think it's necessarily a bad thing. I suppose people just enjoy the memories these evoke. Floppy disks were in some ways not that great. You could easily lose data. It happened to me quite a number of times at university. Still, they had a certain charm to them. You now have so much data;

10.5 - The German produced Tefifon tape cartridge.
Source: Museum of Obsolete Media

10.6 - The MCD cassette (Micro Cassette Disk) from
Hungary. Source: Museum of Obsolete Media

gigabytes stored in the cloud and on devices. Floppies are reminders of a time when things were a lot easier and simpler. Actually, I miss them too, although I don't own any sort of USB sticks shaped like floppies.

FT: Do you think that people will continue to be obsessed with obsolete media when the actual physical objects are no longerm available?

JC: I think there will always be a sense of nostalgia for these objects. I suppose there will come a time when nobody owns old videocassettes anymore, but I think that's still a long way away. The interest might even grow over the next few years, as people realise they really need to sort out the old media they have laying around. Remembering these media is important when reflecting on how we can preserve them, how we migrate their content, and so on. I think obsolete media could become even more important going forward.

FT: Do you collect contemporary media in advance of their inevitable obsolescence?

JC: I do. I sometimes collect objects that are quite current. In a few years, they may very well not be, as we gradually move further and further away from storing data on physical media. I think it's interesting to tell the story of how they came about and how they relate to other formats.

FT: I noticed you award certain obsolescence ratings to particular media on the museum's website. How does this work?

10.7 – A display of Jason's ever-growing collection at the British and Irish Sound Archives conferences in 2018. Photo: Jason Curtis

JC: The ratings were something I did a few years ago. I had seen similar things on other websites where they tell whether a format, like a particular videocassette format, is extinct or endangered. I thought it would be interesting to develop a rating system that considered two kinds of obsolescence: media stability and player availability. You see, some media are likely to lose integrity over the years, while the players are still around, while other mediums might work forever, but there will be nothing to play them on.

FT: **If I remember correctly, the 3.5-inch floppy disk had a two star obsolescence rating, while some of the older or more obscure formats went as far as five stars and are highly endangered. Can you tell us why?**

JC: These floppies are endangered both because there aren't that many left and because there are not a lot of people that own devices that can play them. Because of the age of the disks, there's a high risk of the data not being readable anymore. Also, if it is readable, there might not be the software available to interpret it. Any disks that are still hanging around are going to be difficult to use now. The ratings give you an idea which media are the most urgent to try and migrate or preserve.

FT: You could say that the floppy disk has found a second life, partly because of its continued accessibility through USB floppy drives. This raises a question: Can a medium ever become truly obsolete?

JC: Well, no media format is ever going to completely die. There will always be somebody who has a device capable of reading it. I've posted about objects on Twitter that I thought were long obsolete, but people responded saying that they still use them. There will always be someone who uses a 5.25-inch floppy disk somewhere. Up until recently the US nuclear weapons force used 8-inch disks to store their data on and they worked fine. Because of their rarity, they were unlikely to be copied. It's difficult to define when something actually does become obsolete. I've usually taken it to be either when the device that uses the format stops being commonly manufactured, or when the company that owns the format stops selling them.

FT: What kind of future do you think the floppy disk has?

JC: In terms of floppies being a viable format, I can't see them ever being repurposed or reinvented. Physical media are already disappearing. Netflix, for example,

is taking over DVD and Blu-ray. Gradually we will move further and further away from having anything on physical media.

FT: Is that a good or a bad thing?

JC: It's convenient, I suppose. In that sense, a lot of people are happy with this transition. You can just go to Netflix and find a film you want to watch. But there's still a lot of stuff around on DVD that you can't get on streaming services. I have a large CD collection and I still try and buy things on a physical format, because I don't always want to go online and stream music. But for a lot of people, it's just easy. I suppose it just comes down to what people prefer.

FT: Your collection falls somewhere in the middle of this discussion. It exists both off and online. What is the future of the Museum?

JC: I'll carry on collecting for as long as I can and keep adding things. At the moment, I still have a backlog of items to add, so I will just keep on going. I've started a Patreon page to bring in a little extra money for purchases, but for me it's still a hobby and not a source of income. I quite like that. I'm fully independent and I fund almost everything myself. I can do what I want with the Museum, as long as I maintain a sense of responsibility to my donors and to the collection itself.

'I think the interest in retro computing is growing because people love to look back at simpler times. In the future, computers as we know them will disappear.'

REBOOTING DIGITAL HERITAGE

BART VAN DEN AKKER (NL) is the founder of the Helmond based
Home Computer Museum, a 1 000+ square meter interactive
experience that covers the history of the home computer, from the
very first to modern variants in the late 90s and beyond. Besides
being part of the digital heritage network of the Netherlands,
where old media such as floppy disks can be read and their
data converted to a modern format, the Museum has acquired a
following within the online retro computer scene and assembled
a loyal community that works in the Museum on a daily basis.

> *We wanted to know more about the interesting
> interplay between old and new, online and offline, and
> international and local that takes place at the Museum.
> Are floppy disks the glue that binds it all together?*

Floppy Totaal (FT): Hello Bart, how is life at the Museum at the moment?

Bart van den Akker (BA): It's incredibly busy. Despite not having any visitors, we're actually working six days a week. There are a lot of people doing things, like adding stuff to the Museum, making repairs, and so much more.

FT: Work never stops in Helmond. How would you describe the Museum to someone who has not been there before?

BA: We're an interactive computer museum of about 1 090 square meters. At this moment we have around 400 computers dating from 1975 onwards. All computers are in working order, so visitors that come to the Museum can use them. They are set up in different rooms that are decorated according to the time in which they were used. So, a computer from 1978 is on a desk from 1978 with a chair and wallpaper from the same period. We have about 40 people working in the Museum. Most of them have a form of autism. We help them explore themselves and find a way to cope with the world, the final goal being to help them find a long-term paid job. We also repair old computers and we sell refurbished ones at low prices. Lastly, we do digital heritage. We read and recover a lot of old media using the original systems, including floppy disks. With all the old computers in the Museum, we can run the data on the original software. That's something really unique in the world.

FT: What is your role in all of this?

BA: I clean the toilets and I am the founder of the Museum. For most of the day I work on the website and social media stuff, but I also make time for repairing and reading old data. I do basically the same things that the other people who work at the Museum do.

FT: We were wondering, how did you decide to start the Home Computer Museum?

BA: In 2016, I visited a couple of computer museums and I was really disappointed by them. These museums were just like art museums; you couldn't touch or use the computers on display. One of these didn't even give any information on the machines. It was basically just a storage unit where you paid an entrance fee. These museums didn't have what I was looking for as a collector. So, I drew up a fully-fledged business plan to create my own museum. I decided to focus on reselling and repairing stuff, so it could be financially independent. For all of 2017 I worked on this plan, and in 2018 we opened our doors to the public.

FT: It sounds like you've been interested in vintage computers for quite some time. When did you start collecting them?

BA: Around 2007 I visited a friend who collected game consoles. I was so amazed by his collection that on my way home I told my wife that I wanted to have an old computer again. By 2016 I had 35 computers. I especially love the stories behind them. For every computer I own I know the back-story – why they were made, why the previous owner bought them, and how they were used. As a museum, you should tell these stories. Right now, three years after the opening of the Museum, we have around 2 500 computers. So, we've expanded quite a bit.

FT: You mentioned being frustrated by not being able to interact with the computers in other museums. What do you hope to achieve by providing this experience in your museum?

BA: That's very simple: feelings of nostalgia. Everybody remembers their first computer. It doesn't matter if you were born in the 90s or in the 60s. At some point, you sat behind a computer and you had this feeling that a machine was listening to you. I want each visitor to the Museum to experience this feeling of amazement. That is why we have the rooms set up as they are, to facilitate this nostalgic sensation.

FT: Can you remember the first computer that made you experience this feeling?

BA: My first computer was a Tandy TRS-80 colour computer, which is now in the Museum collection. Actually, most of the computers in the Museum are owned by me personally. The reason for this is that I want the computers to be safe, even if something happens to the Museum as a company. Eventually we will start a new company with the current Museum board members. This company won't do anything besides 'owning' the computers and then rent them out to the Museum. We don't want the computers to be sold in case we go bankrupt. Many people donated computers to us, knowing that we would keep them safe. I feel a lot of responsibility towards them.

FT: Maintaining all these computers can't be easy. Can you tell us a little more about the ways floppies are used in the Museum?

BA: We use them daily; we simply have to. When you install something on an old computer you can't use SD or USB cards. Every time we boot up or check a computer that just came in, we have to start by putting a floppy into it. We want to keep the experience in the Museum as easy as possible, meaning every computer should be on when the Museum opens. Right now, it takes us about 15 minutes to start everything up with at least four people. A lot of computers need an input command to start the software, so we need to install it in a way that it auto boots as much as possible. However, as a visitor, you can still reset the computer and try to load the disks in yourself.

FT: Are there any modern tools you use to make your work easier?

BA: We use a relatively modern laptop to insert data using serial or parallel cables. Another tool that we use is Kryoflux, which

11.1 - Bart van den Akker holding a floppy disk in the workspace of the HelmondComputerMuseum.
Photo: HelmondComputerMuseum

is a device that can connect to all kinds of drives, including those for floppy disks. We mostly use it to read data and turn this into an image file, which we can use and offer for download on our website. You can download the image from there to write your own disk. Or if you don't have the tools, we offer a service where we can send you the original boot disks for any system you want. We don't just automatically share everything we have, though. With diskmags and games there are some copyright issues involved.

FT: It seems like floppy disks are a practical tool to keep the computers in the Museum running. I wonder, are the disks themselves also important to you as cultural artifacts?

BA: Absolutely, I love the sound of a loading floppy disk. The first computer I had, the Tandy TRS-80, didn't have a floppy drive, so I had to work with cassette tapes to load in software, which takes forever. When I got my first computer with floppy drives, which was an Intel 80386, I have these nostalgic memories of going to a friend's house, copying games onto a disk, and then using some kind of archiver, like zip, arj, or Ace, so I could play them again at home. I just love them.

FT: One of the main services that the Museum offers is data recovery from floppy disks and other media. What is the idea behind this and how does this relate to your mission as a museum?

BA: For a long time, at least till the early 90s, most people stored their data on floppies. There were few other options for long-term data storage and the alternatives were really expensive. All kinds of data would be stored on these disks, from poems to the entire picture libraries of an art gallery. The data on floppy disks is heritage and should be rescued. Nowadays, the readers for the 3.5-inch disks are still relatively easy to come by, but for 5.25-inch or 8-inch it is nearly impossible to find a computer that supports them. That's where we come in. We have the hardware to read the data and move it to a USB stick, a Google Drive, or whatever else.

FT: Besides floppy disks, what other kinds of media collections do you have in the Museum?

BA: The Museum contains two large collections. One is the largest big box PC game collection in the world, which is owned by Anne Bras and contains around 2 000 games. The other is our CD-i collection, which is also the largest of its kind in the world. Most of this content is already shared on the Internet, but we are open to any request for a game that we have in our inventory. Last week I received an email from somebody who wanted to have a copy of a staff-training game made by Burger King for the Philips CD-i.

FT: The Home Computer Museum is also part of the Dutch Digital Heritage Network. How did that come about and what does it entail?

BA: In 2020, the Network conducted research in which they found that there was a huge problem at cultural institutes. It turns out that a lot of them have their data stored on old media formats that they can no longer access. This data would likely get lost if nothing is done to address the problem. We got into contact with the Network and showed them how this data could be read and preserved. They were quite amazed by the ease with which we could do it, so they decided to make us part of their network. Eventually, there will be at least three places in the Netherlands where you can retrieve your data: one in Amsterdam, one in Groningen, and the third is us in Helmond. Institutes can call us and we will help them recover their data and give advice on how to store it in future.

FT: **The people who work at the Museum appear to be a close-knit community. Can you tell us a little more about who they are and what motivates them to work at the Museum?**

BA: The main thing is that they all have an interest in computers. Some of them have really excellent hardware knowledge, while others are more into software or web design. We have a broad range of knowledge and skills at the Museum. Everyone is basically from around the Helmond area. However, we also get people from further away who want to work for us for at least a couple of weeks. We now have somebody from England who is planning to come over to the Museum for two weeks as a volunteer. If you love computers and you want to work in the Museum, then you are very welcome!

FT: **Are the volunteers at the Museum accustomed to working with floppy disks?**

BA: It depends on their age. There are people aged over 50 here who used to install Windows 3.1 with floppy disks, and there are 16-year-olds who have never seen a floppy drive before. We have to explain what they are. What we usually do is just show them the Museum, the history of computers, and how floppy drives work. Of course, they still have knowledge of computers, so it's not completely new to them. Everyone working here has their own memories, their own first computers, and their own experiences.

FT: **Another thing the Museum offers is a daytime activity and work reintegration program. Could you tell us a little bit more about that?**

BA: Sure. We don't care about how you have been labelled in the past, as long as you want to work towards a good job in the future. So, we have people that come from many different backgrounds: we have people from foreign countries and we have people that struggle with mental health issues. They used to have a job,but lost their position, because of autism, for example. A lot of companies do not understand how to work with people with autism, so they get very little support and become

11.2 – The museum is home to a wide selection of machines by known and obscure manufactures from the 70s onwards. The collection also contains non-computer objects, like the Sinclair C5. Photo: HelmondComputerMuseum

11.3 – Visitors are able to boot up any plugged in machine and try out their vintage coding or gaming prowess.
Photo: HelmondComputerMuseum

ill. What we do at the Museum is create a safe space, and slowly get our staff back to a 'normal' working pace; like being on time, bringing their own lunch, stopping at some point to go home, etc. We do this in such a friendly way that we've never had anyone leave. We have volunteers now who have been here for more than three years. They stick with us even after they finish their internship and get a job, because they love being here. They might work for 40 hours a week, but still have one day off on Saturday to help at the Museum. Because of this, we can keep helping them after the internship if necessary. When something goes in the wrong direction at their work, we can talk about the problem and support them. In this way we have become a social safety net for many people.

FT: Even though you are based in Helmond, you have managed to reach quite a large international audience through social media. What's the strategy behind this?

BA: When we started the Museum in 2016 I figured that the only way to make a name for ourselves was by using the Internet. I felt that only focussing on the Netherlands would be really limiting. I wanted to share what we do at the Home Computer Museum with the entire world. On Instagram we started posting one picture of a computer at the same time every day. The response was so strong that I decided to share more stories about our computers. Slowly our following grew. Now, when something happens at the Museum during the day, I'm already thinking about how I can turn that into an Instagram post. We also use Twitter and YouTube, and I am now looking into TikTok, Twitch, and even LinkedIn. I've found that on each platform there is someone who likes what we're doing and so we are reaching out to as many people as possible. This also results in more people finding out about us and visiting us in person. I think the worst thing a museum can do nowadays is to not promote themselves online. We currently have over 18 000 Instagram followers, which makes us by far the biggest computer museum on Instagram. Even Bill Gates and Steve Wozniak know about us.

FT: What do you think about the current interest in retro technology? Is there any value in it besides nostalgia? If so, where does this value lie?

BA: I think the interest in retro computing is growing because people love to look back at simpler times. In the future, computers as we know them will disappear. Nobody's buying desktop computers anymore and even if you have a laptop, it is increasingly likely that you have a detachable screen. I think in a few years we will only use our phones. That's all great, but something that people are now realising is how stress free it was to not have constant access to the Internet. You don't have to think about everything that's going on all the time. That's why I think retro is coming back. We had the game development department from the University of Eindhoven come over to the Museum for a tour. At some point I saw

11.4 - A child engaged in discovering the games from his parents' youth. Photo: HelmondComputerMuseum

a line forming in front of our Pong Machine. One student said: 'Sir, this is the most fun game you have over here.' And that's a game from 1972 on a black and white screen.

FT: How do you envision the future of the Museum?

BA: We hope to be open for visitors again soon. After that, we'll try to be an example of how a museum should be run. I think other museums need to understand that they have to generate an income to survive as a company. We are the prototype for the International Council of Museums, and are being sent all over the world as an example.

Perhaps the Computer Museum could even become a franchise, like McDonald's, operating in different countries. In every country there is data stored on media that can't be read anymore. Our digital heritage services could be expanded to the entire world. I think every computer museum should offer services like this. You should be able to go to a museum with your old floppy and let them read it. By doing so, we can keep helping people without relying on subsidy or sponsorships.

FT: As we move further and further away from physical media, what will the digital heritage that you showcase in the Museum mean for future generations?

BA: Digital heritage reveals the way in which things have evolved over the years; how we started computing by using punch cards and how this evolved into what we have today. The way data is stored is mostly the same as back then; it's all 0s and 1s. The floppy was a major storage devices over the years. It started in the 60s with the 8-inch floppy and it carried on until the 2000s with the 3.5-inch. There's a lot of data stored on floppies and there's a lot to know about them. We started with just 90 KB of data stored on a piece of magnetised plastic and this developed into the harder plastic of the 3.5-inch disk. We can show this evolution and people can learn from it. I think that in order to make the future, one must understand the past.

FT: And how about the future of the floppy disk? Is there any?

BA: No, I don't see that happening. The technology itself might have one… perhaps for long-term storage, although the way the floppy stores data is limited to a particular size. Still, unlike CDs, they don't have material inside that can rot and lose data in the process. I haven't seen a properly stored disk that lost any data. If there is a future for the technology it lies in the storage unit itself, the magnetised plastic basically. Whatever the case may be, we will keep showing them in the Museum, and we will store them well. We'll also make sure that we have functioning drives, so that even in many years to come we can read the data from them.

'I think anybody who is putting anything on a floppy in 2020 is absolutely doing it to make a statement.'

FREE RANGE TROUBLEMAKER

JASON SCOTT (US) is a free-spirited archivist, filmmaker, performer, and historian of technology. He is known under the online pseudonyms Sketch, SketchCow, and the Slipped Disk, and has been called a 'figurehead of the digital archiving world'. He works for Internet Archive and has given numerous presentations at technology related conferences on the topics of digital history, software, and website preservation.

We met up with Jason to learn more about his archival work and his DIY approaches to media conservation. Does the future of the floppy disk lie in the hands of enthusiastic 'amateurs'?

Floppy Totaal (FT): Hi Jason, let's get this interview started! Can you tell us something about your many occupations?

Jason Scott (JS): Sure, my main job is being the 'free range archivist' at the Internet Archive in California. This involves a mixed bag of advocacy and public speaking, along with interfacing with customers, patrons, groups, and institutions, all of whom wish to either understand how to use the archive, provide things to it, or make us a part of whatever project they're working on. In other words, I do all the things where pure programmatic web usage can't help.

FT: When did you start working with the Internet Archive?

JS: I started there in March of 2011. The archive at the time had support for software, but only worked with it in a very limited way. They stored files, but they did not do much with them. There had been a couple projects in the 2000s that aimed to preserve old software. Most of these ended up as pallets full of unused floppy disks. Some collections were mirrored from other websites, but with no real analysis or presentation to them. One of my main projects when I started working at the Archive was making software emulation function in the web browser. In the same way that you could play a movie, or listen to music, you could now execute a program or boot a disk in the browser. This set into motion a whole variety of additional projects. As a result, we now have a very large library of software from all sorts of sources, including floppy disks, CD-ROMs, cassette tapes, DVDs, and a whole lot of purely digital files.

FT: How did you end up in this line of work?

JS: In college I used to be a film student. I thought that I was going into movie production, but I ended up not liking the business side of it. Instead, I went into video games, and then moved into being a system administrator for a company in Boston, where I worked on and off for about 13 years. I had a very good salary, and during that period of time, I became more and more interested in doing my own side projects on computer history. Eventually, using my film degree, I made a few documentary films. One of them was *BBS: The Documentary*, which was about the Bulletin Boards systems. Another documentary was called *Get Lamp* and tackled the game genre of text adventure. I was spending my time and money on these projects, gathering more and more old computer material from the 80s and 90s. While doing this, I became known as the person who would speak publicly about older computer subjects and provide context and lore to it. It was only natural that over time the Internet Archive employed me. Some people thought I already worked there, it seemed like such a good match.

FT: One of the things you often talk about is floppy disk preservation. Did you already have a special relationship

with floppies before you started working with them at the Archive?

JS: I've been using floppy disks ever since I was 11 years old, so that's from 1981 onwards. That was my transition year from cassette tape to floppy disk. It was also when I got my own computer at home and at school, which I interacted with using floppy disks. I remember that our teacher at the time handed one disk to each of us, in the way you are handed an important tool. I obviously loved it. A floppy disk was a relatively limited, small, black square that seemed extremely fragile. Of course, it was tougher than it was made out to be, but you couldn't throw a floppy into your back pocket or just leave it in the car. Everything used to depend on these fragile black squares that were not designed to survive in the real world. They were like the opening vanguard into the computer world for so many. So much data still remains stored on these things, while they are now no longer compatible with anything other than outdated machines and systems.

FT: You are working on preserving this early computing history, from the 1980s until the present. This time period corresponds with your teenage years. Is there an element of nostalgia involved?

JS: I've noticed that in recent years there has been more and more of a resistance towards the idea of nostalgia. Usually, it just leads to a discussion of what the term actually means. For me, I think nostalgia involves the portrayal of a past time with an overflowing sense of emotion, and letting everything you interact with from that time – all the evidence, all of the artifacts – be coloured by that. However, lately the novelty of computer history seems to be wearing off, which is the sign of a maturing area. Nostalgia becomes less of an issue. I'm lucky that I lived through the time that I am historically interested in. There are unquestionably things that I have preserved that otherwise might not have been available.

FT: You are known for taking on a DIY approach to archiving. Your Archive Team project pops to mind. Could you tell us a bit about this?

JS: Archive Team originated after noticing that there was a class of material on the World Wide Web that you can call 'user created data', like web pages, forums posts, pictures, and so on, that was getting lost. We started to see more and more situations where users posted content on a whole range of different services. Here, somebody is the caretaker of the user data, but has absolutely no mandate, no guarantee really, on how that data is maintained. A time will come, either quickly or not so quickly, where the host will say that they are no longer interested in maintaining this information and then this data gets lost. My idea was that when it gets announced that a particular service is closing down, a group of people should go in, make copies of all the material, and then maintain it in some way for future reference. That was the fundamental idea of what became Archive Team. When we started out, it was a rather straightforward and loose process. We just jumped into action whenever we became aware that a service started to die. Of course, people had opinions over whether or not it was great that a bunch of amateurs were doing this, but we were not competing with anybody. It just had to happen before the shutdown date.

FT: What is the difference between this rather DIY approach to archiving compared to that of larger institutions? Is there any?

JS: Let me preface this by saying that I am neither a trained, nor a learned archivist. When I speak, I do so from a position of what I have observed over the course of the years. Functionally, there are two kinds of institutions involved in archiving: long term archiving done as part of a larger institution; and groups or institutions that pride themselves in innovation, utilising new mediums and approaches. There's a lot of the first, and not many of the second. When a new medium or a new realm makes itself available, there will usually be a kind of a miss-filing for many years. When the first academic paper on text adventures was written, this was done under Germanic studies, because that was the closest that institutions could get to perceiving what it was. Only over time, will a medium start to gain a foothold as a discipline. My concern however, was that webpages were still very new and extraordinarily

fragile, so archiving them couldn't wait. We can't build a storehouse for webpages and then wait for people to use them. They were going to disappear en masse and very quickly, which is why we jumped in. The timeframes are different in more traditional archives compared to the work we do. I'm so used to literally hour-by-hour deadlines with the Archive Team. I will be told on Wednesday that something is disappearing by Friday.

FT: You actually share your preservation work through several social media outlets. One of the things you do is so-called 'disk reads' of floppy disks that you stream through Twitch. What drives you to do this?

JS: I'm always very interested in odd platforms and grounding them in something they weren't fully designed for. I believe that in the realm of archiving and preserving things, there's a performative aspect. Demonstrations can really add something. I went to a glass museum this month and they have a show where they make something in front of the cameras in 30 minutes. There is a person who's telling you what's going on and they have cameras mounted all over the lab that they switch between, so you can get close-up views of the entire process. Only a tiny fraction of the people in that audience are going to become glassmakers, but it demonstrates to them the meaning and the knowledge behind the discipline. When I do disk reads online these function in the same way. Disk reads are very

12.1 – Jason Scott doing one of this Twitch streams. Here he is working on digitising a collection of VHS films.
Source: Twitch.com

12.2 – A Floppy Disk Flux Image of *The Bard's Tale* - Disk 1, Side B. These sort of images are created using tools like cryoflux. They are visual representations of the magnetic image of the disks. Source: Jason Scott

hypnotically repetitive. You put in a floppy disk and then, using a tool that has some sort of visual feedback, it reads the disk, retrying where it fails, and then it produces a result. I have found that at least a few hundred people enjoy watching me do this.

FT: What kind of reactions do you get? Who watches these streams?

JS: Occasionally, you'll get people for whom floppy disks were never a part of their history. They're very young and have never interacted with these disks. When they see them being read, they're completely confused. Sometimes somebody will get excited about what is going on and they will contact me. Once, somebody was cleaning out a house and found massive amounts of floppy disks that had belonged to his father. So, I was asked if I was interested in taking these thousands of floppies to turn them into disk images. He only knew about me, and the process of disk preservation, because of my online presence. I just love the idea of doing something that appears extremely dull, while interacting with an audience.

FT: It seems like the floppy disk, more so than any of the other old media, has a special appeal that crosses generations. Why do you think this is?

JS: Floppy disks are now such a distant part of how a person interacts with their computer, that their usage and their continued existence represents a fascination in the same way people like printed type or handmade paper. It's a glimpse into a period that's gone. If you look at any old tool, you see how it works and a person can demonstrate that function. What works really well with floppy disks is that you have the initial beauty of the form factor. You have the extra items, the notches, the index hole, the inner band that become like artifacts that describe how they work. Then you get into how the data is preserved on them, which is another discipline entirely. Finally, there's being able to interpret what you read off the disk in such a way that you can recreate it or make it available.

FT: Nowadays, there are still people putting out music or video games on floppy disk. What do you think attracts them to the medium?

JS: I think anybody who is putting anything on a floppy in 2020 is absolutely doing it to make a statement. Like, they want the actual medium of the floppy to be part of the story of whatever they're doing. The idea that you're using this old thing; it's like the difference between sending out an electronic invitation to a party or going through the trouble of having an impact printed business card with a full listing of the party details mailed to everyone's home. A more efficient medium exists, but the older one carries a meaning beyond the data. You offer a mode of a time that's passed, when computers were simpler. You can do interesting things through a lens of reduced capacity; there's a statement there. The medium can speak to people and be explored without it being in competition or influenced by industry. We are currently in a realm where people who are choosing to work with floppy disks are open to some of its oddities, its inconveniences, its problems, but also its uniqueness. It's a joy!

FT: Are these more recent floppy disk endeavours something that would also be potentially interesting to archive at some point?

JS: I personally think that these newer artifacts are just as relevant to save as the old ones and I think that the process for preserving them is pretty simple now. It's not out of the realm of possibility that an artist who is releasing something on floppy disk today is using the same tools that are being used by expert archivists. So, along the way, the person is probably unintentionally already manufacturing an archive of it. I think their stuff is worth saving, because it tells you something about the floppy disk's current position in society.

FT: Can you tell us about the current challenges and advantages of digital archiving?

JS: We now have at our disposal the ability to both ingest an enormous amount of data and run very deep, very involved interpretations of that data in ways that were not possible 40 years ago. For instance, one of the biggest problems we have in tape formats is that these have been known to change every two or three years and afterwards will not be readable. It's not a technical problem, but vendors want to constantly upgrade and control their data. It sets up an endless chase, trying to maintain warehouses of different types of tape drives, keeping them running, just to be able to use that software to pull data from tapes as soon as they become available. But you can also just make a mechanism that slowly reads any tape you put into it and create a massive image of the magnetic data on that tape.

FT: Is this what you are currently doing with floppy disks?

JS: Yes, in essence we are fully imaging the disk. This doesn't mean we've hacked an IBM PC or Apple Disk II, or something. We're just reading the data down to the microscopic level agnostically, completely from the ground up, and then writing more and more complicated software to pull in all of the data. We do this up to the point that we can recognise when different manufacturing methods were used and detect tear and damage on the disk. We are able to visually see where magnetics have gone off and do multiple reads to average them out. This helps us figure out what the long-faded byte was, like you would with a photograph. That's where we're heading. It takes an enormous amount of energy and processor time to do this, but it gives me hope that we're not taking things down in terms of months or years. If we get really good reads, we can just keep revisiting these.

12.3 – A promotional meme for Achive Team.
Source: Archive Team

12.4 – The logo for the 'Archive Team Warrior' tool.
Source: Archive Team

FT: Do these readings always succeed? Is there such a thing as a completely unreadable floppy disk?

JS: That's a hard question. So far it has been ultimately possible to recreate and get all the data off most floppies. However, you have to make changes to the incoming data to make them readable. There are very few where we couldn't at least read the format, and then interpret what we're looking at, but of course, this does not produce a 100% correct copy. There are protection schemes that are so hostile to being copied, that they won't even work with the original disks on the original hardware. It all boils down to what is readable and what is not readable.

FT: What is the legal aspect of copying all these floppies?

JS: There are very few companies that have an overriding interest in old floppy disk software, but there are some. In general, they will contact us and ask us to not make a certain image available. We will usually take it out of public distribution, although we will keep our own copies. I don't think there was ever someone who said we couldn't keep a copy of the material. The whole microcomputer industry, of which floppy disks are a part, is so many generations beyond what it was back then, that there really isn't much in the way of huge problems in terms of ownership. This is especially so because it is clear we are working from an archival and preservation angle, and the material isn't being remixed into a new commercial product. So, I don't really pay much attention to the legal concerns. I'm almost completely focused on the purely physical challenge of acquiring as many floppy disks as possible.

FT: What happens to the disk after the imaging is done?

JS: The disks that I image are stored at the Internet Archive in very large boxes, inside of larger boxes, inside of a warehouse. They're marked as imaged and stored away. I don't believe in throwing them out, unless we get a situation where we have to. Thankfully, right now, I work for an institution where the amount of space taken up by piles of floppy disks is minuscule compared to many of the other materials that come in. Of course, not everybody works like this. I have certainly dealt with people who have imaged floppies and then thrown them out or dropped them off with other people to write over them. You know, people will do what they do.

FT: Do you think there will come a moment when all the floppies from the 1980s and 90s are archived? Will your work ever be done?

JS: I think that you have to look at it in stages. Floppy disks represent the time period when everything was being stored on them, right? So, that means a certain corpus of data is being pulled off floppies.

Some of this data is personal, some of it is commercial, some of it is very rare, and some of it is ubiquitous. We are still, in the present day, finding new data locked away on floppies that we never had before. Sometimes they would do runs of a 1 000 to 2 000 floppy disks, and then they would make changes and put out another 1 000. You wouldn't notice that these are completely different if you didn't look at them closely.

FT: Is it really that important to have all these different versions of outdated software?

JS: It's nice to have and nice to do. We have more than enough data that's pulled from floppy disks to have a reasonably good, general image of what life on floppy disks was like. I would estimate we have probably anywhere between 1 million to 1.5 million different floppy disk images out there in the world. If, however, your entire thesis rests on having access to a particular floppy disk, well, you might miss out. There might still be something out there that needs to be found. I consider floppy disks to be folk art. There are works that were created by folks in the early 80s that would be passed around and copied between user groups and individuals. These were stored on CD-ROM compilations or put into very large archive files that were then put on FTP sites for people to download. We are now focusing on stuff that, for various reasons, just missed out on getting that extra leap to greater distribution.

FT: Do you think floppy disks will continue to find much use in the future?

JS: Well, at some point they will fall off the list. Right now, floppy disks usage reduces every day. It will continue to fade as the first go-to medium, but maybe it will find other uses. I think with floppy disks we now have a unique historical opportunity. There is an enormous amount of interesting data stored on them. We are grabbing as much of it as we can, using very advanced tools. We are discovering some really interesting sub stories, like how they were made, mistakes that were done, common changes, how vendors worked, and all these are nice to have. Also, we have a body of people who are excited when a new discovery is made or something new comes out. There is an audience for early computer history. For now, floppies are still part of the conversation.

MEDIA GLOSSARY
by Jason Curtis

B

1.44 Megabytes (MB)
This is the formatted capacity of a 3.5-inch High Density floppy disk and is usually abbreviated to 1.44 MB. The High Density version of the 3.5-inch floppy disk was introduced in 1987, and was identified by an extra hole in the opposite corner to the write-protect notch.

286
The Intel 80286 microprocessor was a 16- bit chip that first saw major use in the IBM PC/AT from 1984. It could offer up to double the speed of the Intel 8086 or 8088 chip and could make use of up to 16 MB of RAM, though in practice, computers of the time never had this much memory.

3-inch floppy disk
The 3-inch floppy (or 'Compact Floppy') was introduced in 1982 and was used in a number of home computers. It had a rigid casing like the 3.5-inch floppy disk, but with a more complex shutter design and independent write-protect switches for each side. It was never as popular as the 3.5-inch floppy disk and died out in the early 1990s.

3.5-inch floppy disk
This was the most popular design of floppy disk. Sony introduced a version of it in 1982 before it was improved upon by the Microfloppy Industry Committee. Initially holding just 360 KB, capacity increased over time with a High Density version holding 1.44 MB in 1987, and a less common Extended Density version holding 2.88 MB in 1991.

486
The Intel 80486 or i486 was a 32-bit microprocessor introduced in 1989, with the first PCs using it that same year. Clock speeds ranged from 16 MHz to 100 MHz, and different versions were available such as the popular 486DX2, running at 66 MHz. The 486 was partly superseded in 1993 by Intel's Pentium range, but it was Intel's Celeron processor of 1998 that became a direct replacement.

4K
4K (sometimes also called Ultra High-Definition or UHD) refers to a horizontal resolution of around 40 00 pixels, and is used in digital broadcasting (though its use in broadcasting is still limited), cinema, and video streaming services such as Netflix and Amazon Prime.

5.25-inch floppy disk
First introduced in 1976 as a more compact version of the 8-inch floppy disk, the 5.25-inch disk was the main type of floppy disk used in the early and mid 1980s, until overtaken by the 3.5-inch disk in the late 1980s. It was truly a floppy disk, as the outer casing was a flexible envelope.

720 Kilobyte (KB) double density disk
720 KB was the capacity of the 3.5-inch floppy disk in its double-sided/double-density (DS/DD) version

introduced in 1984. The capacity was different if a disk was formatted for an Apple Macintosh, where it could store 800 KB, or for a Commodore Amiga, where it could store 880 KB. The High Density version of the 3.5-inch floppy disk was introduced in 1987 and offered 1.44 MB of storage, soon replacing the DS/DD version.

8-inch floppy disk

The first type of floppy disk, introduced by IBM in 1971. Initially designed as just a bare disk, by the time of its commercial launch it was enclosed in a fabric lined flexible plastic envelope. It was replaced by the 5.25-inch floppy and died out in the early 1980s.

A

Amiga

The Amiga was a family of personal computers produced by Commodore between 1985 and 1994. Offering a graphical user interface, pre-emptive multitasking, and good graphics and audio capabilities, it was a popular system in the late 1980s and saw use for applications such as gaming and desktop video editing.

Apple Disk II

The Disk II floppy disk drive was released in 1978 for the Apple II computer, and used 5.25-inch soft-sectored floppy disks. Up until this point, the main means of saving information on the Apple II was by much slower cassette tape. Initially offering a capacity of 114 KB, Disk II capacity later increased to 140 KB. The drive came with a controller card that was fitted into an expansion slot in the computer, to connect to the external drive via a ribbon cable.

Arduino

Formed after an education project that started in 2005, Arduino is an Italian company that makes inexpensive single-board microcontrollers that can be used in digital projects, in a similar way to Raspberry Pi. All Arduino hardware and software is licensed under open source.

Arri Alexa

The Alexa is a range of professional digital video cameras, first introduced in 2010. The series is widely used in the film industry and uses memory cards such as SxS or Cfast, or external SSD drives such as SXR, for storing recordings.

ASCII code

ASCII (American Standard Code for Information Interchange) is a way of representing characters such as letters, numbers, punctuation, and some control codes in 7-bit binary code. The first version of the standard was published in 1963. It was developed from earlier standards for telegraph communications. In ASCII code a capital A is represented by 1000001. Extended ASCII uses 8-bits and allows for an additional 128 characters such as accented letters, more mathematical symbols, and some drawing characters.

Atari 1040ST

Atari's ST range of computers was launched in 1985, with the 1040ST being introduced in 1986 with 1 MB of RAM. It was the first personal computer to offer this much memory as a standard. It came with a graphical user interface and MIDI ports, which made it popular for use in the music industry. The 1040ST came with a built-in 3.5-inch floppy disk drive, but as this was not a High Density drive, it offered only 720 KB per disk.

B

Bandcamp

Bandcamp is a website set up in 2008 that allows people to upload recordings, such as music or podcasts, that users can then download or stream. The owners of the recordings can set their own prices, with Bandcamp taking a cut.

BASIC

BASIC (an acronym for Beginners' All-purpose Symbolic Instruction Code) is a computer programming language. It was first released in 1964 and was designed to be easy to use. Many variants of BASIC were used on home computers of the late-1970s and 80s.

BBS (Bulletin Boards systems)

A text-based online community system popular before the widespread availability of the World Wide Web. A BBS could be run from someone's home computer, with other users dialing in via a modem. The first BBS, the Computerized Bulletin Board System (CBBS), was launched in 1978. Usage of BBS systems reached a peak around 1996 before quickly declining. Some still operate today and are accessed via Telnet or SSH.

Betamax

An early analogue videocassette format aimed at the consumer market. Introduced in 1975 by Sony, it competed in a 'format war' with the VHS video format for a number of years, before Sony conceded in 1988 and began to produce VHS video recorders as well. Sony continued to make Betamax video recorders for the Japanese market until as late as 2002.

Big box games

Refers to computer game software packaged in cardboard boxes, mostly from the 1980s and 90s, when computer games came on physical media such as floppy disks or cassette tapes, and often included printed manuals. Boxes generally became smaller in the early 2000s, and then were replaced by standard DVD cases. Big box computer games are prized by retro videogame collectors.

BitTorrent

BitTorrent is a means of sharing large files, such as software, video, or audio, through a peer-to-peer protocol. There is no central file store, and users install client software to enable them to download files from other users' computers. Files are downloaded from multiple computers in small pieces to speed up the process and distribute the load. These fragments are later reassembled by the BitTorrent client. The BitTorrent protocol has been used for piracy, but also has legitimate uses for distributing content.

Blu-ray Disc

Blu-ray Discs were introduced in 2006 and offer high-capacity storage for high-definition video, video games, data, or audio. They offer around five times the capacity of a DVD by using a shorter wavelength blue laser. Blu-Ray took part in a brief format war with the HD-DVD format that lasted until 2008. Recordable and rewritable versions are also available, known as BD-R and BD-RE respectively.

C

CD

Short for Compact Disc, an optical disc format for digital music introduced in 1982. Developed jointly by Sony and Philips, the Compact Disk was partly based on the earlier LaserDisc format. By 1988 CD sales had overtaken those of 12-inch vinyl LPs and went on to sell billions of copies. However, in 2020 the value of CD sales in the US fell below those of LPs. The Compact Disc was developed into formats such as CD-ROM, and recordable versions were available as CD-R and CD-RW.

CD-ROM

CD-ROM (Compact Disc Read-Only Memory) is a data storage format that was introduced in 1985 and based on the audio Compact Disc. Initially offering a capacity of 650 MB, a single CD-ROM disc could hold the contents of over 900 3.5-inch floppy disks. Writeable versions such as the CD-R and CD-RW came later.

Compact Cassette

Often called cassettes, or simply tapes, the Compact Cassette was introduced by Philips in 1963. It saw off competition from other similar cassettes, partly due to Philips freely licensing the design. It became one of the dominant formats for music distribution in the 1980s and 1990s. Besides being used for music distribution, the Compact Cassette became a popular low-cost format for home computer data storage in the 1980s, albeit with a reputation for poor reliability.

Compaq

Compaq was a US computer company formed in 1982, and one of the first to sell an IBM PC compatible computer in the form of the 1983 Compaq Portable – possible because Compaq was able to legally reverse-engineer the IBM BIOS. Compaq went on to sell IBM PC compatible desktop systems under the Deskpro brand including the Deskpro 386 – the first desktop to use the Intel 80386 chip. Compaq merged with Hewlett-Packard in 2002, and the Compaq name disappeared in 2013.

CompactFlash

Introduced in 1994, CompactFlash is a memory card format that was widely used in digital photography, and is still used in digital SLR cameras where its larger physical size compared to other memory cards such as Secure Digital is not an issue.

CPU

A computer's CPU or Central Processing Unit executes the instructions to run computer operating systems and programs. In modern devices it consists of a microprocessor. Modern microprocessors might have several processors or 'cores'.

Cybersquatting

Also known as domain squatting, it is the practice of buying a domain name that is identical or very similar to that of a business, organisation, or person, usually with the idea of making money by asking for large sums to sell it. Username squatting on social media is a similar practice.

D

DevOps

DevOps is a model of software development where development and operations teams work together throughout the life cycle of a software product. It is related to the Agile model of software development, and is designed to make software development faster and more reliable. A key feature of DevOps practice is to do small but frequent updates rather than big releases.

Discord (software)

Discord is a service that allows for text, voice, and video communications. It is organised on the basis of 'servers' or communities, and each server can have multiple channels. Since its inception as a platform for gamers, it has begun to move towards more general use.

Disk Image

A disk image is an exact copy of the contents and file system of a piece of media, such as a hard disk, floppy disk, optical disc, or data tape. A disk image can be treated by a computer as a virtual disk, but is usually read-only. An ISO file or image is a specific type of disk image for an optical disc.

Diskmag

Diskmag is a name given to computer magazines published on floppy disk, containing articles, software, and sometimes multimedia. Different magazines were made for different platforms, such as the Apple II, Commodore 64, Apple Macintosh, and IBM-compatible PCs.

Doom

Doom is a video game series first introduced in 1993 for IBM PC compatible computers. It is considered one of the earliest first-person video games. Over the years it has been updated and made available for a number of operating systems and video game platforms, with the latest version being *Doom Eternal* released in 2020 and available for Microsoft Windows 10, PlayStation 4, Xbox One, and the Nintendo Switch. Besides videogames, the Doom franchise has included books, movies, and comics.

DVD

DVD (Digital Versatile Disc) is an optical disc format initially introduced for video playback in 1996, but later used for software and audio. It quickly replaced the VHS video format, offering higher quality and interactivity, as well as cheaper players. Recordable (DVD-R and DVD+R) and rewritable versions (DVD-RW and DVD+RW) came later. Sales of DVD-Video discs are declining in the face of competition from both Blu-ray Discs (which offer high-definition video) and streaming video services.

E

eBay

Originally founded as an online auction website in the US called AuctionWeb in 1995, eBay (as it became known in 1997) has grown to become a multinational shopping and auction company with over 1.5 billion listings as of June 2020. The story about the trading of Pez sweet dispensers being the reason for its founding is a PR fabrication.

eBook

Electronic books are readable on dedicated eBook readers, or on other devices such as PCs or smartphones. They may have a print equivalent, or be solely published in electronic form. eBooks are usually available to be read online, or downloaded to a device, often with some form of digital rights management (DRM). Some earlier eBook systems such as Sony's Data Discman relied on physical media for distribution.

F

FFmpeg

FFmpeg is a command-line open-source suite of software, first introduced in 2000, for converting, processing and editing audio and video files.

Flash Media

Media using flash memory. These store information without the need for power (also known as non-volatile memory). Examples include memory cards, USB memory sticks, and solid-state drives (replacing hard disk drives).

Flex Diskette

This was the name used by Dysan for the 3.25-inch floppy disk, produced by them and a couple of other manufacturers for a few years after 1983. The 3.25-inch disk looked like a smaller version of the more common 5.25-inch floppy disk, and like the larger disk, had a flexible outer cover. Competing against more popular designs of floppy disk, the 3.25-inch disk was a commercial failure and is now rare.

Floppy diskettes / disks

Refers to any disk with a flexible magnetic disk inside a cover. The first floppy disks were the 8-inch and 5.25-inch designs, and these had a flexible outer cover. Later designs, like the ubiquitous 3.5-inch floppy, had a rigid cover, but still had the flexible disc inside and so the name continued to be used.

Flux

Refers to magnetic flux, the means by which data is stored on magnetic disks such as floppies. Systems such as KryoFlux enable the recovery of data from different sizes and formats of floppy disk by reading the flux transitions and storing the results as raw data that can be used as disk image.

FTP

FTP (File Transfer Protocol) is an Internet protocol developed in the 1970s that is still used for the transfer of files, for example to upload web pages from a PC to a web server. Although some browsers offer some support for FTP, it is more generally used with FTP client software to set up the connection and manage files. A secure version is also available, called SFTP (SSH File Transfer Protocol).

GIF

GIF or Graphics Interchange Format was developed by Compuserve in the late 1980s as a means of distributing images over the Internet at a time when connections were mostly by modem. It is a lower-quality image format than the later PNG, but it is possible to create animated GIFs, which are widely supported and very popular.

GitHub

GitHub is a hosting service for developers to store source codes and enable collaboration with features such as version control. It hosts commercial software projects, as well as open- source. Begun in 2008, it was acquired by Microsoft in 2018.

GPS

The Global Positioning System is a US-operated navigation satellite system for geolocation. Other navigation satellite systems with global coverage are operated by Russia, China, and the European Union.

H.264

H.264 is a video compression standard that is also known as Advanced Video Coding or

MPEG-4 AVC. Developed by the JVT (Joint Video Team) Project in 2003, it is (as of 2021) one of the most commonly used compression formats, supporting up to 8K resolution.

HandBrake (software)

HandBrake is an open-source tool first developed in 2003, for ripping and converting video files to different formats.

Hasselblad

A Swedish camera manufacturer known for its high-quality medium-format film cameras that are popular with professional photographers. Hasselblad cameras were used by NASA on its Apollo missions to space. More recently, the company has moved into making digital medium-format cameras.

I

IBM 5150

Launched in August 1981, the IBM Personal Computer 5150 was the first IBM PC. Using an Intel 8088 processor and the MS-DOS operating system (branded as IBM PC DOS), it came with up to two 5.25-inch floppy disk drives and either 16 or 64 KB of RAM. The IBM PC quickly became a standard, and dominated the personal computer market along with its many clones.

Intel 80386

The Intel 80386 or i386 was a 32-bit microprocessor introduced in 1985. Its first major use was in the Compaq Deskpro 386 of 1986, an IBM-compatible PC launched over six months before IBM launched their own model of PC using the 386 chip.

Internet Archive (archive.org)

A non-profit organisation and digital library founded in 1996. It provides access to archived copies of websites (through its Wayback Machine), software, music, movies, magazines, and books, which it digitises through a network of 33 scanning centres. It also advocates for a free and open Internet.

IP address

IP stands for Internet Protocol. Each device on a network has an IP address. These can either be static and unchanging, or dynamically allocated as needed. There are two versions in current use – IPv4 and IPv6.

iPod

A range of popular portable music players that was introduced by Apple in 2001, the iPod has been through a number of generations, and has used both small hard-disk drives and flash memory for storing music. The iPod Touch model is still available as of 2021, but is no longer a dedicated music player.

ISA card

An ISA (Industry Standard Architecture) card is an expansion card for PCs that could add functions such as sound card, modem, or network ports. Originally introduced for the IBM PC in 1981, ISA card slots were still included in PCs until the early 2000s, despite being just 8- or 16-bit.

ISO file

An ISO file is a copy of the contents and file system of an optical disc such as a CD-ROM or DVD in a single file, usually with a .iso file extension. The ISO name relates to the file system used by optical discs, ISO-9660, first defined by the International Organization for

Standardization in 1988. An ISO file can be treated by a computer as if it were an actual disc.

K

Ko-fi
Ko-fi is a site for creators to receive donations, either one-off or regularly. It does not (as of 2021) charge any fees and aims to be a kind of online tip jar. The name is a pun on the word 'coffee'.

KryoFlux
KryoFlux was developed by the Software Preservation Society and is a floppy disk drive controller board and software that enables the recovery of data from different sizes and formats of floppy disk. It works by connecting a working floppy disk drive via the KryoFlux board to a computer, reading the flux transitions, and storing the results as raw data that can be used as a disk image.

L

LaserDisc
First introduced in 1978 as DiscoVision, the LaserDisc was an optical disc format for analogue video aimed at the consumer market. Unlike Betamax and VHS, it lacked the ability to record, but offered higher quality video and eventually, digital sound. The most common size was 12-inches in diameter, but 8-inch and even 5-inch LaserDisc variants were also available. Pioneer continued to produce LaserDisc players until 2009, though the last LaserDisc titles were released in 2001.

Linux
An open source computer operating system first released in 1991 by Linus Torvolds and based on the Unix system from the 1970s. Originally designed for personal computers, Linux now powers most of the world's servers and the Linux-based Android operating system that powers many of the world's smartphones.

M

Macintosh
The Macintosh range of computers was introduced by Apple in 1984, and while not the first computer system to use a graphical user interface, it was the first commercially successful one. Macintosh computers are now called Macs by Apple, and continue to be sold. Initially, Macintosh computers used 3.5-inch floppy disk, but in 1998 with the launch of the iMac, Apple began to remove floppy disk drives from its computers.

Mattel Aquarius
A very short-lived home computer, introduced and then quickly discontinued in 1983. With poor graphics and limited memory, it was dubbed 'the system for the seventies' by some Mattel staff. Like some other home computers of the time, it offered software on ROM cartridges as well as cassette tapes.

MCD (Micro Cassette Disk)
Not a cassette at all, but an early floppy disk design from Hungary, first invented in 1973 and way ahead of its time. Looking like a 3-inch Compact Floppy, it had a robust casing and offered up to 150 KB capacity. It wasn't sold commercially until the early 1980s however, by which time it faced competition from other floppy disk designs.

MIDI

MIDI (Musical Instrument Digital Interface) allows computers and mobile devices to communicate with digital musical instruments such as drum machines, sequencers, and synthesisers. It's a widely used protocol, and the first devices to use it were introduced in 1983.

Model M keyboard

A PC keyboard introduced in 1984 by IBM that many people feel is one of the best computer keyboard designs ever, despite its weight and noise, which it makes up for with durability and feel. It uses a buckling spring design, using a spring to press a lever to operate the electrical switch for the key. Slight variations were produced over the years, and a version of the Model M is still produced as of 2021 by Unicomp.

MOD files

Originating on the Commodore Amiga computer in the 1980s, MOD files (also known as module files, MOD music, or tracker music) contain information for the playback of digital music. Because MOD files contain both sequencing information and samples of the sounds that are being used, they could be described as a mix of MIDI and WAV file. There is a MOD scene subculture of people who create, exchange, and listen to the files.

MP3

A standard for digital audio. Most of the development of MP3 was carried out by the Fraunhofer Society in Germany. It is a lossy compression format, and was designated as MPEG-1 Audio Layer III in 1993, and later MPEG-2 Audio Layer III by the Moving Picture Expert Group in 1995. The a cappella version of the song *Tom's Diner* by Suzanne

Vega was used to refine the compression algorithm. MP3 playback is still widely supported, but it is not considered a high-quality format.

MPEG

The term MPEG usually refers to video files with a .mpeg or .mpg extension, usually in MPEG-1 or MPEG-2 format, which despite being an older compression format, is still widely used and supported. MPEG is also the Moving Picture Expert Group. Set up in 1988, this body has set standards for many audio and video file formats and compression methods. Besides MPEG-1 or MPEG 2, these include MPEG-4 (often called MP4) for video, and MP3 for audio.

MS DOS

MS-DOS (Microsoft Disk Operating System) was a command-line computer operating system first used on the IBM PC in 1981. It underpinned early versions of the Windows graphical user interface up until Windows ME.

Museum of Obsolete Media

Curated by Jason Curtis, a librarian from the UK, the museum was founded in 2006 as a collection of media formats, covering video, audio and data storage, and later film formats. The museum website was created in 2013 and provides information and photographs for the over 700 formats currently in the collection as of 2021.

Networked CD-ROMs

CD-ROM drives can be shared across a local network. This is useful, for example, in a library situation where a database runs from a number of CD-ROMs in a CD-ROM tower, connected via a SCSI cable to one PC on a network, allowing the database to be accessed from a number of PCs. The advent of online databases made this facility largely redundant.

Nintendo Game Boy

The Game Boy was a popular handheld video game console, introduced by Nintendo in 1988 Initially with a monochrome screen, it added colour graphics in 1998 before being replaced by the Game Boy Advance console in 2003. The Game Boy used small ROM cartridges for games and its cartridge slot could also be used for accessories like the Game Boy Camera and the Game Boy Printer.

NTSC

The NTSC (National Television System Committee) standard was used in analogue television broadcasting in the North and Central America, parts of South America, and some Asian countries from 1954, when it was introduced for colour broadcasting. It offers lower resolution than PAL, at 525 scanning lines.

O

Open source software

Open source refers to software where the source code is available to inspect, modify, or share. Many people may have contributed to the development of open source software. Examples include Linux and Open Office. Open source does not necessarily mean the software is free, and there could be charges for training or hosting. Likewise, free sofware is not necessarily open source

P

Packard Bell

Originally a US radio manufacturer formed in 1933, the brand was resurrected in 1986 by Israeli investors to market their value IBM-compatible personal computers. Packard Bell became a subsidiary of NEC in the late 1990s, and since 2008 has been a subsidiary of Acer. Packard Bell computers are marketed in Africa, Europe, and the Middle East. Packard Bell is headquartered in the Netherlands. There is no connection between Packard Bell and Hewlett Packard.

PAL

PAL (Phase Alternating Line) was an analogue broadcasting standard for colour television, and was used across much of Europe and Africa, some of South America, and many Asia-Pacific countries. Coming later (1967) than the NTSC standard, PAL offered a higher resolution, at 625 scanning lines.

Patreon

Patreon is an online service developed in 2013 for creators to make income from their work in the form of regular subscriptions from patrons. Patrons may receive benefits such as early access to content, access to discussion forums, or even merchandise. Creators can specify different tiers of benefits, depending on the level of subscription.

PCI slot

PCI (peripheral component interconnect) expansion slots allow hardware to be connected to a PC's motherboard. Introduced in 1992 and eventually replacing older types of expansion slots, such as ISA, they allowed the addition of items such as hard disk controllers, sound cards, and modems. Faster expansion systems such as PCI-Express have super-seded it, but PCI slots are still found in desktop PCs.

PDP-10

Digital Equipment Corporation's PDP-10 range was a mainframe computer system, popular with universities. Introduced in 1966, it was one of the computers that formed the basis of ARPANET, the fore-runner to the Internet. Later called DECsystem-10, it was discontinued in 1983.

Philips P2000C

The P2000C was a portable computer, one of a range of P2000 computers produced by Philips in the early 1980s. Whilst it was sold as a portable device, it was mains-powered, and heavy. It incorporated two 5.25-inch floppy disk drives and ran CP/M, but could run MS-DOS with the use of an optional CoPower card.

Printed circuit board

Printed circuit boards or PCBs are used in almost all electronic devices. They route electricity to components mounted on the board via a series of copper pathways. PCBs can be multi-layered, with copper layers on both sides and even within the board. Components can be attached to the board using older 'through hole' technology or by means of the newer surface- mount technology, which avoids the need to drill into the board.

Punched cards

Used for data storage and processing since the 1890 US census, the punched card (also known as IBM cards or Hollerith cards) is a piece of card with holes punched in it to represent data. They became popular for use with computers, and their usage continued to be widespread until the 1980s. There are variations in size and numbers of columns between cards, but they all follow the same principles. A standard 80 column punched card contains 80 bytes, so 99 981 boxes of 2 000 cards would be required to contain the same amount of data as a single 16 GB microSD card.

Q

QIC Minicartridge

A magnetic tape cartridge for data storage, mostly used in the 1980s and 90s. QIC stood for Quarter Inch Cartridge and referred to the width of the tape. The QIC Minicartridge was one of a family of QIC formats. Its smaller size meant it was often used in PCs, since the drive could fit into a floppy disk drive bay.

QWERTY

An arrangement of keys on a keyboard, QWERTY describes the first five alphabetic keys on the top row. Introduced in 1870, it was intended to prevent the type arms on manual typewriters from clashing by moving the most commonly used letters away from each other. Other keyboard layouts have been tried, but the dominance and familiarity of QWERTY layouts have ensured its survival, despite it no longer being necessary.

R

RAM

Random Access Memory is a computer's working memory, which can be read or written to very quickly. It is usually volatile, meaning this data gets lost when the device is switched off. A typical desktop PC in 2021 has 8 GB of RAM, whereas the IBM PC came with as little as 16 KB when launched in 1981.

Raspberry Pi

A small, inexpensive, single board computer, which was originally designed for educational use, but is also used for purposes such as home automation and robotics. Made by the Raspberry Pi foundation in the UK, they have become the best-selling British computer ever.

RCA SelectaVision

Also known as the CED Videodisc or Capacitance Electronic Disc, SelectaVision was a brand name for RCA's failed attempt to market a consumer analogue videodisc system. Launched in 1981, it used a finely grooved vinyl disc in a caddy that was read by a stylus. Although discs and players were inexpensive to manufacture it had to compete with LaserDisc and videocassette systems such as VHS and Betamax. It was withdrawn in 1986.

ROM cartridges

ROM (read-only memory) cartridges were a popular way to store games for video game consoles, but have also been used for home computers and PDAs, as well as some other devices. They had the advantage of instant loading, and made pirating software more difficult. Because of their manufacturing costs and limited capacity, video game consoles moved to optical discs during the 1990s, while only handheld game consoles continued using them.

S

Secure Digital (SD) card

The original SD memory card was introduced in 1999 and was intended for use in devices such as digital cameras and PDAs. Smaller variants have been introduced since – miniSD (now obsolete) and microSD (often used in mobile devices). Newer standards, like SDHC and SDXC, provide higher capacities and speeds to cope with high-definition video.

Sharp Pocket Computer

Sharp made a range of pocket computers in the 1980s. These were 8-bit machines that could be programmed using BASIC, and had a range of accessories available such as a printer, tape drives, and a floppy disk drive. The disk drive used a proprietary Sharp Pocket Disk that could hold just 128 KB.

Sharp Pocket Disk

This small 2.5-inch floppy was designed for use with the Sharp Pocket Computers of the mid-1980s. It resembled a smaller version of the standard 3.5-inch floppy disk, but was double-sided, offering 64 KB per side.

SID music

The Sound Interface Device was the sound chip found in the Commodore 64 home computer of the 1980s. It was a three-voice synthesiser module that could be programmed using BASIC or machine code to create music for computer games. Music made using SID is still produced, and there is a vast library of SID music available that can be played with suitable software.

Sinclair ZX81

The ZX81 was Sinclair Research's second entry into the UK home computer market. It was also produced for the US market by Timex under license. As the name suggests it was introduced in 1981. Initially coming with just 1 KB of RAM, black and white graphics, and a membrane keyboard, it was inexpensive and proved popular despite its limitations. Software was loaded via slow and sometime unreliable cassette tape.

Sony Mavica

Sony first demonstrated a prototype Mavica camera in 1981. This model used a 2-inch floppy disk (Video Floppy) to record up to 50 analogue video images. The Mavica line was subsequently launched in 1987 and initially used the Video Floppy, but went on to be a true digital camera line that used 3.5-inch floppy disks as well as 8cm CD-R and CD-RW disks until the early 2000s.

Sony HiFD

One of a number of attempts in the late 1990s to replace the 3.5-inch floppy disk, Sony's HiFD (High capacity Floppy Disk) offered capacities of up to 200 MB, while the HiFD drives could still read standard floppy disks. It wasn't a success in the marketplace. Competition from the Iomega Zip drive, and CD-R/CD-RW drives spelled the end for the medium.

Sneakernet

Refers to the physical transfer of data from one computer to another without using a network, for example by floppy disk, CD- ROM, or USB drive. The 'sneaker' part of the name refers to the US term for running shoes or trainers. It is used where there is no network available, or where there are security concerns with transferring data over a network.

T

Tandy TRS-80

The original TRS-80 was a home computer introduced in 1977 by Tandy. It was one of the most successful early microcomputers, with a large software library. Initially using cassette tapes to load software, a 5.25-inch disk drive, and eventually an external hard disk drive later became available. The TRS-80 Model II was an incompatible version aimed at the small business market, and the TRS-80 Colour Computer was another later incompatible variation, introduced as a cheaper home computer to compete with the Commodore VIC-20.

Tefifon

A West German analogue format for music from the 1950s and 60s, the Tefifon used cartridges containing an endless loop of plastic tape with grooves on it that was played by a stylus. Sound quality was reasonably good, but the format didn't catch on with record companies. Three different size cartridges were available, offering between 18 minutes and 4 hours of music.

Tracker

Originating on the Commodore Amiga computer in 1987, a tracker (or music tracker) is software for creating digital music that contains samples plus the sequencing information. A tracker can work with multiple channels of sound, or tracks, and uses MOD files (also known as module files, MOD music, or tracker music) to store output. Tracker software became available on IBM-compatible PCs in the 1990s, as sound cards became widespread.

U

USB

USB, or Universal Serial Bus, enables connections between devices to communicate with each other, provide power or both. Its first notable use was on the Apple iMac of 1998, which included USB 1.1 ports, but did away with an internal 3.5-inch floppy disk drive. Various faster versions of USB have been introduced since, along with many different connectors.

USB floppy drives

Drives for 3.5-inch floppy disks that can be used as external devices connected via a USB cable. They were first necessary for anyone wanting to use floppy disks when Apple removed floppy disk drives from the iMac in 1998, but are still available to purchase as of 2021.

U

VCR (Video Cassette Recording)

The Philips VCR format was an early analogue domestic videocassette format that was introduced in 1972 with the N1500 videocassette recorder. Mostly found in Europe, it initially offered recording times of up to 60 minutes, with the VCR-LP (long play) version introduced in 1977, offering up to 180 minutes. It was discontinued in 1979 when Philips and Grundig introduced the Video 2000 format.

VHS (Video Home System)

VHS was not the first domestic videocassette system when it was first launched in Japan in 1976. Despite this, it was by far the most successful and saw off competition from Betamax and (to a lesser extent) Video 2000 in the 1980s. It was extended into camcorders as the smaller VHS-C, a higher-quality S-VHS variant, and even a digital HD version as D-VHS (or D-Theater for pre-recorded releases). With the coming of DVD, its days were numbered. The last major film to be released on VHS was in 2006.

Video CD

Launched in 1993, Video CD was based on the Compact Disc. With digital compression it could store 74 minutes of video in a quality that was comparable to VHS. Lacking copy protection and easy to copy onto CD-R or CD-RW, it was unattractive to film studios, and the coming of DVD spelt its end during the 2000s, although it remained popular in Asia and developing nations.

VM (virtual machine)

A computer within a computer, a virtual machine can be used, for example, to run a different operating system or emulate different hardware, without affecting the host systemWWW. They can also be used for testing purposes or sandboxing, with the computing resources allocated to the 'guest' system kept separate. Multiple virtual machines can run on the same host.

W

Wi-Fi

Wi-Fi is a means of wireless local networking using radio waves. First widely offered in the Apple iBook of 1999, it is now used across a wide range of devices, from laptops and mobile phones to, more recently, fridges and light bulbs (the so-called 'Internet of Things'). Various different versions of the family of IEEE 802.11 standards have been developed over the years to allow faster connections.

Windows XP

A graphical user interface operating system for personal computers, Windows XP was released by Microsoft in 2001. Unlike previous versions of Windows, XP did not sit on top of MS-DOS. Various versions of XP were available, including Professional and Home versions, as well as Media Center and Tablet PC editions. Extended support ended in 2014 and only a very small number of devices still use Windows XP.

xD card

Developed jointly by Olympus and Fujifilm, the xD-Picture card was a compact memory card introduced in 2002 for use in digital cameras. It was more expensive and less successful than other memory card formats such as Secure Digital (SD), which were also used in devices other than cameras. By 2010, Olympus cameras all offered Secure Digital or Compact Flash slots, and xD was effectively obsolete.

Yamaha OPL3 SA3 Sound chip

The OPL3-SA3 was an audio chip made by Yamaha and used in sound cards in the 1990s. The SA3 was the third-generation of the OPL3 chip and added 3D sound capability on top of features from the previous generation SA2 chip,such as a CD-ROM interface and 'plug and play' capability.

Z

Zenith Minisport

Launched in 1989 by Zenith Data Systems, the Minisport was a very small notebook computer running MS-DOS. It used a unique floppy disk design called the LT-1, a 2-inch disk capable of

holding 793 KB. Although the LT-1 was based on the Video Floppy disk, it was incompatible. An optional external 3.5-inch floppy disk drive was available.

Zip disk

Iomega's Zip disk and drive were introduced in 1995. The disks were a type of floppy disk, but larger and thicker than a standard 3.5-inch floppy disk and so the drives could not read standard floppies. Despite this, Zip was briefly successful and the initial capacity of 100 MB was increased to 250 MB and then 750 MB. There were some reliability issues, in particular the drive failure dubbed the 'click of death', and sales dropped after 1999 as it faced competition from CD-R and CD-RW disks, followed by USB flash drives. The Zip range was discontinued in 2006.

**Onomatopee 197: 'Floppy Disk Fever:
The Curious Afterlives of a Flexible Medium'**

ISBN 978-94-93148-86-4

Publisher:
Onomatopee
Lucas Gasselstraat 2a
5613 LB Eindhoven

Text and Editing: Niek Hilkmann
Design: Thomas Walskaar
Foreword: Lori Emerson
Media Glossary: Jason Curtis
Copyediting: Oliver Barstow
Typesetting: Simon Browne

Interviews: Niek Hilkmann
and Thomas Walskaar
Support: Lídia Pereira (*Rebooting Digital
Heritage* and *The Main Event*)

Feedback: Aymeric Mansoux, Florian
Cramer, Freek Lomme, Lídia Pereira,
Silvio Lorusso and Luca Ménesi

Printer:
AS Printon (Tallinn, Estonia)

Typset in:
Worksans by Wei Huang
BitPap by Cile

Print run:
2 000 copies

This book was made possible in
part by Creative Funds NL

**creative industries
fund NL**

www.floppydiskfever.org

ACKNOWLEDGEMENTS

This book wouldn't be possible without the kind contributions by Lori Emerson, Tom Persky, Florian Cramer, Clint Basinger, Nick Gentry, Foone Turing, AJ Heller, Joerg Droege, Adam Frankiewicz, Jason Curtis, Bart van den Akker and Jason Scott.

Equally important were the feedback and inspiration we received from the artists who were part of the Floppy Totaal events at WORM, including Graham Boosey, Kai Nabuko, Sascha Müller, Ogon Uru, Apatt, Jan Miversen, Floppy Kick Records, Bass-O-Matic, Eoforwine, Dr. Kondor, Irrlicht Project, Back To The Fucking Future, Dennis de Bel, Holy Void, O900 Isopod, The Cryovolcano, Remute, Michael Ridge and Kisszanto.

We would like to acknowledge the various institutions and venues that hosted and/or were interested in our project, including Varia, WORM, Zinecamp, V2, Onomatopee, the Institute of Network Culture, the Piet Zwart Institute, and the Rietveld Academy.

Last, but not least, we'd like to compliment you for picking up this book and reading through these credits. Thanks a dozen!

NOTES